PREPARING LEGAL DOCUMENTS

PREPARING LEGAL DOCUMENTS *Nonlawyers* CAN READ AND UNDERSTAND

WAYNE SCHIESS

Defending Liberty
Pursuing Justice

Cover design by ABA Publishing.

Printed in the United States of America

10 09 08 5 4 3 2 1

Library of Congress Cataloging-in-Publication Data

Schiess, Wayne, 1963–
Preparing legal documents nonlawyers can read and understand / by Wayne Schiess. — 1st ed.
p. cm.
Includes index.
ISBN 978-1-59031-964-2
1. Legal composition. I. Title.

KF250.S349 2008
808'.06634--dc22

2008023998

Discounts are available for books ordered in bulk. Special consideration is given to state bars, CLE programs, and other bar-related organizations. Inquire at Book Publishing, ABA Publishing, American Bar Association, 321 North Clark Street, Chicago, Illinois 60654-7598.

www.ababooks.org

This book is dedicated to my mother,
Alyce Carol Brimley Schiess.

There's an old story told by some who preach about plain English.

A woman approached the elevator in a fancy hotel and asked the attendant, "Is this elevator ascending or descending?"

"I'm sorry, ma'am, but you'll have to ask at the front desk about that," he replied. Then he called out, "Going up!"

It's a nice story that conveys this simple message: speak in language your audience can understand. Imagine my pleasure to have been present when a similar incident occurred.

"For the meeting, do you require assistance in providing enhanced capacity?"

"I don't know about that, but we need your help to set up more chairs."

That's what this book is about.

No, not chairs or meetings, but communicating plainly, so people can understand.

CONTENTS

INTRODUCTION

The Audience for Plain Legal Writing

Picture that real person, baffled by legalese. Exasperated. Think of that person when you write a legal document for nonlawyers.

Too many legal documents intended for nonlawyers are dense, archaic, and unnecessarily complex. In truth, they simply contain traditional legalese: jargon, terms of art, long sentences, and complicated syntax. What's more, these documents sometimes contain mistakes of English and sometimes of substantive law, both of which are harder to spot and fix because the text is written in traditional legalese. Ultimately, these documents fail in their essential purpose: to communicate binding legal content to a nonlegal reader.

We can do better, and that's the goal of this book: to teach you how to convey binding legal content, in writing, to nonlawyers.

The audience for plain legal writing

In this book, the focus is on the audience of nonlawyers. Keep that in mind. Picture your grandmother if you have to, but break the habit of writing for the general public the way you write for other lawyers. Remember, the nonlawyers reading your text have widely varying levels of education, from a Ph.D. to a grade-school education. For so wide an audience, aim a bit low. I often aim for a 10th-grade reading level, and when the context is particularly important, I try to go even lower: I once revised a set of jury instructions to a 7th-grade level.

I aim below the likely reading level because that helps the audience. You see, nonlawyers are often not at their best when they are reading legal documents. They read under stress, with negative emotion, with preconceived ideas and confusion. They read in fear. Here's a taste of what it's like for them:

> **RELEASE**
>
> KNOW ALL MEN BY THESE PRESENTS, that I/we Linda Smith residing at 1000 Amber Lane, Emmett, ID, the undersigned, First Party, for and in consideration of the sum of FIVE THOUSAND AND NO/100 Dollars ($5,000.00) to me/us in hand paid by Real Insurance, Inc. and John James, Second Party, the receipt of which is hereby acknowledge, I/we being of lawful age, for myself/ourselves, my/our heirs, administrators, executors, successors and assigns hereby remise, release, acquit and forever discharge the said Second Party, his/her, their, and each of their heirs, executors, administrators, successors, and assigns and any and all other persons, partnerships, associations, and/or corporations, whether herein named or referred to or not, of and from any and every claim, demand, right, or cause of action of whatever kind and nature, either in law or equity, especially liability arising from an accident which occurred on or about 08/11/2005 at or near the following location INTERSTATE 100, DOWNTOWN, USA for which I/we have claimed the said Second Party to be legally liable, but this release shall not be construed as an admission of liability.

The woman who received this and forwarded it to me was an English teacher with a master's degree, and I expected a complaint about the writing or a critique of the word usage. Even the typos. But she did not point out how badly written it was or complain that it contained typographical errors and archaic legalisms. No. What she asked was, "Should I sign this? What does it mean?"

There was confusion and frustration in her voice. Even for an English teacher, the legal language was overwhelming.

With this kind of legal text, the "baffle factor" is high. Surely anyone reading it—even a lawyer—can see that. So why do we write that kind of dense legalese for nonlegal readers?

Why we don't write well for nonlawyers

Maybe we haven't been taught. I surely wasn't taught the skill in law school—almost no lawyers were. And even today I teach plain legal writing to only a small percentage of law students, those who take my advanced courses.

Maybe we're stuck in the habit of "writing like a lawyer," which usually means our writing is excessively formal. One of the main things I strive to get across in my courses and will strive to get across in this book is that to adapt to the nonlegal audience, you must change your outlook completely. You must think about communicating the ideas as clearly and simply as you can. You must elevate the importance of the expression of the ideas to the same level as the importance of the substance of the ideas.

Maybe we're afraid of sounding unsophisticated. To communicate with nonlegal readers, you'll need to write in a voice that is closer to spoken English, or what we might call a colloquial tone. For nonlawyers, a colloquial tone is not only good, it's necessary. It may be foreign to you now, but you can learn. You can learn to invite the reader in. You can abandon the fear that it won't sound legal. You can abandon the approach of writing to impress. This book will teach you how.

After all, what you're writing is important stuff.

The documents nonlawyers need to read

Many, many legal documents are intended for the nonlegal audience. Here are just a few examples of documents that nonlawyers should be able to read and understand:

Apartment leases
Basic contracts
Consumer regulations
Credit-card agreements
Employee manuals and handbooks
Homeowner's association bylaws
Insurance policies

Jury instructions
Opinion or advice letters
Public notices
Releases
Software licenses and user agreements
Website disclaimers
Wills

And more—any legal content for nonlawyers, generally in a consumer transaction, but also communication between people and their government. These documents affect rights and liabilities and have as their primary, intended audience the general public—nonlawyers.

Do you write any of those kinds of documents? If so, this book is for you.

CHAPTER 1

Forms and a Plain-Drafting Process

Question your forms. Master them. Then plan and prepare a plain-English document.

The realities of forms

Nearly all plain legal drafting results from converting an existing form into plain English. Of course, there are times when you will be drafting from scratch. If so, apply the principles in this book to produce plain legal drafting. But if, as is usually the case, you are using a form, keep in mind some key advice.

First, although you may be able to rely on a form for substantive content, you should almost never rely on it for the expression of the content. Most forms are, by their very nature, outdated. Many, in fact, contain dreadful legalese, archaic word usage, and other drafting errors. Question everything about a form, but especially the language.

Second, apply your drafting skills to a form as carefully as you would when drafting from scratch. Forms tend to induce haste, laziness, and complacency. Be sure you know all the content, and be sure you revise the form appropriately for your current transaction. In other words, master the form. For more on the challenges of using forms, see Chapter 3.

Third, have the guts to cut. Nearly all form documents grow by accretion. They almost never shrink. Typically, the drafter will think that any provision that was useful on the last transaction can't hurt this transaction, and so the accreted provisions multiply. For plain legal drafting, you must cut the provisions that aren't necessary or that do not relate to your transaction.

With these attitudes and approaches in mind, you are ready to prepare a plain-English document by revising a traditional form.

A process for plain-English revising

Once you have a reliable form to use for your transaction, how should you go about revising it into plain English? I recommend a five-step process.

Step 1 Read the entire document from beginning to end. You are trying to get a sense of the content and complexity of the text. This is hard for most lawyers, because even though it's helpful to read straight through without stopping, lawyers have an editor's mentality. We want to mark it up. Okay, a little marking won't hurt now. In fact, I often find myself highlighting words and phrases and taking brief notes at this stage.

Step 2 Create a list of the substantive content. I do this by creating a separate document called "[name of document] content." My content document is nothing more than an exhaustive list of every substantive item in the original. I create this content document for two reasons: (1) to help me master the content, and (2) to use as a checklist when I produce a revision. I use the checklist to be sure that my revision contains the same content as the original. (Remember the underlying premise of this book: It's about the language, not the substance. In my plain-English work, I keep the substance the same to the greatest extent I can.)

Step 3 Sort and order the content list. Think about the needs of the reader, the most important topics in the document, the order in which the transaction will be carried out, and other considerations. Group related concepts together and begin thinking about headings, subheadings, and numbering. Feel free to question and change the order of the original.

Step 4 Rewrite the text in plain English, applying the principles in this book. In revising, I often work directly from my sorted content list, keeping the original document handy as a reference. This approach helps free you from the original language, which is probably poor, but it keeps you closely tied to the original content.

Step 5 Revise and edit your new document. Naturally, the basic principles of editing apply here. Try to give yourself some time away from the document before you edit; this distance will allow you to bring a fresh perspective to the text. Devote a substantial amount of time to the edit; experts recommend as much as 50 percent of the total time on the project. Ask others to read and comment on the text; include one lawyer who is an expert on the subject and one nonlawyer who is unfamiliar with the subject. (You may decide to test the document on its intended audience. See Chapter 7 on testing.)

An example of the process

The following text is excerpted from a real class-action notice. The names have been changed. Given that this notice was sent to ordinary consumers, most of whom have no legal training, I think the writing here is particularly poor. It is complicated, legalistic, poorly designed, and uninviting.

We can take this text through the five-step process for converting to plain English.

Step 1 Read the entire text from beginning to end.

Pardon my commentary in the bullets—I couldn't help myself.

Original class-action notice

TO: ALL RECORD AND BENEFICIAL HOLDERS OF THE COMMON STOCK OF ETRA, INC. (THE "COMPANY"), INCLUDING ALL OF ITS PREDECESSORS, DURING THE PERIOD BEGINNING ON AND INCLUDING JANUARY 1, 1995 THROUGH AND INCLUDING MARCH 22, 2007.

- Is a nonlawyer going to understand what record holders are? Beneficial holders? The all-caps text makes it hard to read.

PLEASE READ THIS NOTICE CAREFULLY AND IN ITS ENTIRETY. YOUR RIGHTS MAY BE AFFECTED BY THE LEGAL PROCEEDINGS IN THIS LITIGATION. BROKERAGE FIRMS, BANKS, AND OTHER PERSONS OR ENTITIES WHO ARE MEMBERS OF THE CLASS IN THEIR CAPACITIES AS RECORD OWNERS, BUT NOT AS BENEFICIAL OWNERS, ARE DIRECTED TO SEND THIS NOTICE PROMPTLY TO BENEFICIAL OWNERS.

- In this paragraph, we mix an instruction to read the document carefully with an instruction to brokers and other agents who, given the subject matter, are certainly more sophisticated than the typical readers. That's confusing. Notice that we have switched from "holders" to "owners." Why? And more all-caps text.

The purpose of the notice is to inform you of this lawsuit (the "Action"), a proposed settlement of the Action (the "Settlement"), and a hearing to be held by the Circuit Court (the "Court"), on October 5, 2007, at 1 p.m. (the "Settlement Hearing"), at which the Court shall consider for approval: (i) whether this Action will be certified as a class action, for settlement purposes only, pursuant to Rule of Civil Procedure 23; (ii) whether the terms and conditions of the Settlement are fair, reasonable, adequate, and in the best interests of the Class and the Company; (iii) whether the Final Order should be entered dismissing this Action with prejudice as against Plaintiffs and the Class, releasing the Settled Claims, and enjoining prosecution of any and all Settled Claims; (iv) the award of Plaintiffs' counsel's attorneys' fees and expenses as provided for herein, as to which award Company has agreed to pay $7.5 million; (v) any objections to the Settlement; and (vi) such other relief as the Court may deem necessary and appropriate. Any of the dates set forth herein may be modified by the Court without further notice. The Court reserves the right to approve the Settlement at or after the Settlement Hearing with such modifications as may be consented to by the parties to the Stipulation and without further notice to the Class.

- This long and dense paragraph is difficult to read and understand. It uses too many defined terms; in fact, it uses some terms that have not been defined: Final Order, Plaintiffs, and Stipulation. It is unnecessarily formal in tone and uses legalistic Romanettes for numbering.

THE DESCRIPTION OF THE ACTION AND THE SETTLEMENT WHICH FOLLOWS HAS BEEN PREPARED BY COUNSEL FOR THE PARTIES. THE COURT HAS MADE NO FINDING WITH RESPECT TO SUCH MATTERS, AND THIS NOTICE IS NOT AN EXPRESSION OR STATEMENT BY THE COURT OF FINDINGS OF FACT.

- Highly legalistic in tone, and using some insider jargon: *such, findings of fact*. Again, the use of all-caps text is unnecessary.

Step 2 Create a list of the substantive content of the document.

Here is my list of the substantive content divided into single-sentence concepts.

- Addressing the record and beneficial owners of Etra and its predecessors' stock from January 1, 1995 to March 22, 2007.
- Instruction to read the notice carefully and fully. The hearing described here may affect your rights.
- Instructions to brokers and agents who hold Etra stock as record owners to forward this notice to beneficial owners.
- Inform you of this lawsuit, a proposed settlement, and a hearing.
- Details of the hearing: held by the Circuit Court on October 5, 2007, at 1 p.m. Items the court will consider:
  - whether to certify a class action for settlement under Rule 23;
  - whether the terms of the settlement are fair, reasonable, adequate, and in the best interests of the class and the company;

  - whether to dismiss this case with prejudice, release the settled claims, and enjoin pursuit of settled claims;
  - whether to award Plaintiffs' lawyers fees and expenses of $7.5 million as agreed by the company;
  - objections to the settlement;
  - other relief the court decides is necessary and appropriate.
- The court may change the dates without notice.
- The court can approve the settlement at or after the hearing and may make changes with the parties' consent without notice to the class.
- The lawyers prepared this document, not the court.
- The court has not made any findings of fact.

Step 3 Sort and order the content list.

The order of the original was good. I agree that we should begin with an address to those receiving the notice, and an instruction to read it carefully seems important to have up front too. Plus, an instruction to brokers and agents to inform beneficial owners should be near the top as well. I will leave those parts intact.

1. Addressing the record and beneficial owners of Etra—and predecessors'—stock from January 1, 1995 to March 22, 2007.
2. Instruction to read the notice carefully and fully. The hearing described here may affect your rights.
3. Instructions to brokers and agents who hold Etra stock as record owners to forward this notice to beneficial owners.
   - It is also hard to quibble with the order of the next section: stating the purpose of the document, the date of the hearing, and then the details of the hearing—this seems a logical order. But I might adjust the order of the items just a bit. Possible dismissal ought to come first, I think. And objections to the settlement ought to come after consideration of the other aspects of the settlement.

4. Inform you of this lawsuit, a proposed settlement, and a hearing.
5. Details of the hearing: held by the Circuit Court on October 5, 2007, at 1 p.m. Items the court will consider:
6. whether to dismiss this case with prejudice, release the settled claims, and enjoin pursuit of settled claims;
7. whether to certify a class action for settlement under Rule 23;
8. whether the terms of the settlement are fair, reasonable, adequate, and in the best interests of the class and the company;
9. objections to the settlement;
10. whether to award Plaintiffs' lawyers fees and expenses of $7.5 million as agreed by the company;
11. other relief as the court decides is necessary and appropriate.
12. The court may change the dates without notice.
13. The court can approve the settlement at or after the hearing and may make changes with the parties' consent without notice to the class.
14. The lawyers prepared this document, not the court.
15. The court has not made any findings of fact.

Step 4 Rewrite the document in plain English.

Now I will rewrite the text in plain English without making substantive changes. If you think I have failed in some way, remember: that's a criticism of my ability to replicate difficult content, not a criticism of plain English.

First revised class-action notice

If you owned common stock in Etra, Inc. between January 1, 1995, and March 22, 2007, you may have rights in a class-action lawsuit.

Read this notice carefully—it affects your rights.

Brokers and agents: forward this notice to beneficial owners of Etra common stock.

This class-action lawsuit may be settled. This notice explains the details and how you can participate if you want to.

The judge will hold a hearing about the settlement on October 5, 2007. At the hearing, the judge will consider these things:

- whether to dismiss this lawsuit and prevent the plaintiffs from suing again;
- whether to approve this lawsuit as a class action;
- whether the settlement is fair, reasonable, adequate, and in the best interests of the class and Etra;
- whether there are any objections to the settlement;
- whether to give the plaintiffs' lawyers $7.5 million in fees and expenses—which Etra has agreed to pay;
- anything else the judge thinks is appropriate.

The judge can change the dates without notice, and the judge can approve the settlement at the hearing or later. If the parties agree, the judge can change the details of the settlement without notice to the class.

The lawyers prepared this document, not the judge. The judge has not made any decisions yet.

Step 5 Revise and edit the document.

For this final edit, I will reformat the text for emphasis and to highlight key information. The final form of this revision also implements techniques recommended by the Federal Judicial Center in its sample class-action notices.

Final revised class-action notice

If you owned stock in Etra, Inc. between January 1, 1995, and March 22, 2007, you may have rights in a class-action lawsuit.

- **Read this notice carefully—it affects your rights.**
- **Brokers and agents: forward this notice to beneficial owners of Etra stock.**

This class-action lawsuit may be settled. This notice explains the details and how you can participate if you want to.

The judge will hold a hearing about the settlement on October 5, 2007. At the hearing, the judge will consider these things:

- whether to dismiss this lawsuit and prevent the plaintiffs from suing again;
- whether to approve this lawsuit as a class action;
- whether the settlement is fair, reasonable, adequate, and in the best interests of the class and Etra;
- whether there are any objections to the settlement;
- whether to give the plaintiffs' lawyers $7.5 million in fees and expenses—which Etra has agreed to pay;
- anything else the judge thinks is appropriate.

The judge can change the date without notice, and the judge can approve the settlement at the hearing or later. If the parties agree, the judge can change the details of the settlement without notice to the class.

The lawyers prepared this document, not the judge.

The judge has not made any decisions yet.

Now that we have a process in place, we can begin studying the specific techniques that will help us make the document readable and plain.

CHAPTER 2

Designing Plain Legal Documents

Abandon the relics of the typewriter. Design text for easy reading and easy skimming.

The way your document looks will either invite readers into the document or put them off. The way your document is presented will either allow them to read it quickly and easily or make their eyes and minds tired. The way your document is designed will either discourage or encourage skipping and skimming—the way we all read. This chapter acknowledges the way readers read and presents some basic principles of modern, professional document design.

Fonts

The two most important types of fonts you will use in documents for nonlawyers are serifed fonts and sans serif fonts.

Serifed fonts have serifs, or small extensions, at the ends of the strokes. These serifs make each letter distinct and allow the eye to seize upon these distinctions more quickly, thus easing the reader's way. Common serifed fonts are

- Times New Roman
- Century Schoolbook
- Georgia

Because serifed fonts are generally regarded as the easiest to read when printed on paper, the main body of your text should probably be in a serifed font. Take a look at the books, newspapers, and magazines you read each day. The main text in most of these publications is in a serifed font.

The next type of font you will use in documents for nonlawyers is sans serif. Sans serif fonts do not have serifs at the end of each stroke, and they generally look more modern and informal than serifed fonts. Some common sans serif fonts, shown here in boldface, are

- **Arial**
- **Century Gothic**
- **Tahoma**

Sans serif fonts are generally considered easier to read on the computer screen than serifed fonts because screen resolutions make the serifs harder to see. If you know your legal document will be read primarily on the screen, you may want to use a sans serif font.

Is it okay to use more than one font in a single document? Yes it is, and one good recommendation is to use a serifed font for the main text and a sans serif, boldface font for the headings. This creates a strong contrast between the headings and the main text, making the headings stand out and allowing the reader to skim the headings more easily. That is the practice used in this book.

A final note: The one mistake that no modern legal writer should make today is to use a Courier font. Courier is a relic of the typewriter. It uses a lot of space on the page and looks old-fashioned.

Type styles

Many legal documents use ALL-CAPS TEXT and underlining. For readable and skim-able documents, you should abandon all-caps and underlining. These two type styles were used when lawyers prepared their documents on typewriters. Typewriters could not create boldface (I guess you could pound the keys really hard) or italics, so we used all capitals in place of boldface and underlining in place of italics. We did this to mimic the type styles used in professionally printed documents.

Today, word processors allow us to accurately mimic the type styles of professionally printed documents. So modern legal documents should avoid vestiges of the typewriter: Use boldface and italics in place of all capitals and underlining.

Besides, all-capitals text is off-putting, difficult to read, and may come across as shouting to today's reader. Underlined text is also more difficult to read than regular type, at least partly because the underline obscures descending letters.

For more information on the vestiges of the typewriter in modern documents and what you can do about it in your own documents, see

- *The PC is not a Typewriter* by Robin Williams
- *Painting with Print: Incorporating Concepts of Typographic and Layout Design into the Text of Legal Writing Documents*, 2 J. ALWD 108 (2004) by Ruth Anne Robbins

Creating emphasis

In many legal documents, especially those aimed at nonlawyers, certain parts of the text must be emphasized, or presented in a way that is conspicuous. In many of these documents, lawyers try to achieve conspicuousness and emphasis by using all capitals. Although all capitals certainly draw the reader's attention because they stand out from the rest of the text, once the reader tries to read the text, it'll be slow going. Better to put the conspicuous text in boldface type.

If the original text looks like this,

> THE HOLDER ASSUMES ALL RISK AND DANGERS INCIDENTAL TO THE GAME OF BASEBALL INCLUDING SPECIFICALLY (BUT NOT EXCLUSIVELY) THE DANGER OF BEING INJURED BY THROWN OR BATTED BALLS AND AGREES THAT THE PARTICIPATING CLUBS, THEIR AGENTS AND PLAYERS ARE NOT LIABLE FOR INJURIES RESULTING FROM SUCH CAUSES.

then you should use boldface instead:

> **The holder assumes all risk and dangers incidental to the game of baseball including specifically (but not exclusively) the danger of being injured by thrown or batted balls and agrees that the participating clubs, their agents and players are not liable for injuries resulting from such causes.**

If other provisions in the document are in boldface type, or if the headings in the document are in boldface type, boldface alone may not satisfy someone who is persnickety about emphasis—a court, for example. So when I want to create conspicuous text, I generally use three techniques at once: boldface type, smaller type size, and a box or a pair of horizontal lines.

I lay out the text like this:

The holder assumes all risk and dangers incidental to the game of baseball including specifically (but not exclusively) the danger of being injured by thrown or batted balls and agrees that the participating clubs, their agents and players are not liable for injuries resulting from such causes.

Some may complain that to make text conspicuous, you should not make it smaller than the surrounding text, but what is important for conspicuousness is contrast. To enhance the contrast, my approach uses three design elements: the horizontal lines draw attention to the text, the boldface type makes the text stand out from the surrounding text, and the smaller type size contrasts this text with the surrounding text.

Line length

If the document is to be readable and skim-able, a line of text across the page cannot be too long. Generally speaking, experts recommend line lengths between 45 and 65 characters. There are usually no settings on a word processor to control the line length, so you have to eyeball it. The longer the line length, the harder it is for your eye to move back to the left margin after reading a line. That's your clue.

The line length, of course, depends on the margins of your document and on the type size. The default settings on most word-processors—1-inch margins left and right and a type size of 12 point, Times New Roman font—create line lengths that are too long. To improve the look of my documents, I usually move my margins in to 1.25 inches on the left and right and increase my Times New Roman font size to 13 points. But you have other options. You can use a font that takes up more space than Times New Roman, such as Century Schoolbook or Georgia.

Suppose you need to get a lot of text onto a single page—maybe the client wants the entire document to fit on one page. Making the type very small will make it hard to read, right? Perhaps, but a lot of it has to do with line length. Newspapers use very small type and get away with it. How? By shortening the line length dramatically with columns. You can break a document into two columns and use a much smaller type size because the line lengths will still be manageable.

Text in a very small font, like 9 points, with a long line length looks like this:

Disclaimer

The holder is admitted on condition, and by use of this ticket agrees, that he will not transmit or aid in transmitting any description, account, picture or reproduction of the baseball game or exhibition to which this ticket admits him. Breach of the foregoing will automatically terminate this license.

The holder assumes all risk and dangers incidental to the game of baseball including specifically (but not exclusively) the danger of being injured by thrown or batted balls and agrees that the participating clubs, their agents and players are not liable for injuries resulting from such causes. The management reserves the right to revoke the license granted by this ticket.

This text can still be readable if you use columns, like this:

Disclaimer

The holder is admitted on condition, and by use of this ticket agrees, that he will not transmit or aid in transmitting any description, account, picture or reproduction of the baseball game or exhibition to which this ticket admits him. Breach of the foregoing will automatically terminate this license.

The holder assumes all risk and dangers incidental to the game of baseball including specifically (but not exclusively) the danger of being injured by thrown or batted balls and agrees that the participating clubs, their agents and players are not liable for injuries resulting from such causes. The management reserves the right to revoke the license granted by this ticket.

Note: I do not recommend columns for a document that is to be read on the screen. It gives you a headache when you have to scroll up and down repeatedly.

By the way, if you look at a single-spaced document with 1-inch margins on the left and right and Times New Roman 12-point type, it will surely look dense and crowded. As I have said, pushing the margins in to 1.25 inches left and right and increasing the type size to 13 points will greatly improve the readability of the document, at least partly because it will shorten the line length. But lawyers have been doing something else to eliminate the crowded look of the default settings: double-spacing.

I do not care for double-spacing; it uses more paper, lengthens the document, and makes it hard to skim. Besides, I am able to read books, magazines, and newspapers quite easily, and none of them are double-spaced. So I do not recommend double-spacing for plain-English documents.

Justification: center, full, and left

Generally speaking, you should not center the text in a typical legal document. It is simply too hard to read. In fact, even headings should be placed on the left margin; that makes the document easier to skim because all the headings line up.

The real question is whether you should left justify or fully justify your documents. Fully-justified text tends to look neater on the page because there are clean vertical lines on the left and right margins. Most books, magazines, and newspapers are fully justified, and your word processor is capable of fully justifying your text.

The drawback of using full justification is that your word processor is not as sophisticated as the programs used for the professionally printed documents you usually read. If you fully justify your legal documents, you will often see odd gaps and spaces in the text. Of course, you can improve the look of the justified text by using the hyphenation function, which breaks words at the right margin and inserts a hyphen. But this can be tedious because you need to be sure that every broken word is correctly hyphenated between syllables.

Here's my advice: if the fully-justified text looks neat and clean and does not have odd gaps or spaces, then full justification is appropriate. Otherwise, left justification, leaving a ragged right margin, is entirely appropriate for legal documents.

Numbering

In transactional documents, a comprehensive numbering system can be useful for readers, especially if the document is long. The numbering provides a sense of priority and order and makes it easy to refer to any specific provision in the document. I recommend numbering for any long transactional document. In numbering your document, be sure to number every separate section, paragraph, and clause in the document. Do not leave unnumbered or "dangling" text.

Not every document needs a numbering system. Many short consumer-transaction documents are better without numbering, and court documents and letters generally do not need numbering. In these documents, numbering tends to make the document seem more formal and cluttered.

If you are going to use a numbering system, I offer three suggestions:

First, do not use Roman numerals (I, V, X, etc.) or Romanettes (i, v, x, etc.). These lend an air of formality to a plain-English document that is not called for. If your document has a lot of numbering, Roman numerals will eventually become hard to decipher. Besides, we have a perfectly good system of numerals, called the Arabic system (1, 2, 3, etc.).

Second, use tabs moderately and combine tabs with hanging indentations to keep the document neat and readable. For example, this text has too many tabs and no hanging indentation:

> **1. Disclaimer**
>
> 1.1 The holder is admitted on condition, and by use of this ticket agrees, that he will not transmit or aid in transmitting any description, account, picture or reproduction of the baseball game or exhibition to which this ticket admits him. Breach of the foregoing will automatically terminate this license.

This text looks better and is easier to read:

> **1. Disclaimer**
>
> 1.1 The holder is admitted on condition, and by use of this ticket agrees, that he will not transmit or aid in transmitting any description, account, picture or reproduction of the baseball game or exhibition to which this ticket admits him. Breach of the foregoing will automatically terminate this license.

Third, use a sensible numbering system. I like this one:

1.	(Topic)
1.1	(Section)
1.1(A)	(subsection)
1.1(A)(1)	(paragraph)
1.1(A)(1)(a)	(clause)

This numbering system gives you five levels for the document. If you need more than five levels in your document, the document is probably too complex or you are over-subdividing it. For more on numbering your document, see Chapter 4.

Initial capitals

Don't use initial-capitals to create emphasis in text, like this:

> The Holder Is Admitted on Condition, and by Use of this Ticket Agrees, That He Will Not Transmit or Aid in Transmitting Any Description, Account, Picture or Reproduction of the Baseball Game or Exhibition to Which this Ticket Admits Him. Breach of the Foregoing Will Automatically Terminate this License.

Reserve initial capitals for titles, proper nouns, and defined terms.

Footers

In a multi-page document, it's helpful to include a running footer. The text of the footer could contain the document's title or description and a page number. The page number display might also contain an "of page" designation: 3 of 6, 4 of 6, and so on. The footer might also contain a file name for internal use.

Endnotes and footnotes

Transactional documents rarely contain citations to authority, and almost never contain endnotes or footnotes. If you are writing a court document or letter, try to avoid using endnotes and footnotes. If you must, footnotes are better. Although footnotes force readers to nod their heads up and down, endnotes are worse because they force readers to flip back and forth between the text and the end of the document.

Tables

Using graphics in your text can ease the reader's way. One especially helpful technique is the if–then table.[1] The if–then table makes it easier for the reader to understand choices and see the options. Here is a good example:

1. Thomas A. Murawski, *Writing Readable Regulations* 39–41 (Carolina Academic Press 1999).

If the number of books sales is	Then the royalty percentage is
1–499	10%
500–999	15%
1000 or more	20%

An example—before

The following example contains many document design weaknesses:

- use of Courier (an outdated typeface)
- use of all-capitals type for emphasis
- use of centered headings
- use of underlining

DISCLAIMER

The holder is admitted on condition, and by use of this ticket agrees, that he will not transmit or aid in transmitting any description, account, picture or reproduction of the baseball game or exhibition to which this ticket admits him. Breach of the foregoing will automatically terminate this license.

THE HOLDER ASSUMES ALL RISK AND DANGERS INCIDENTAL TO THE GAME OF BASEBALL INCLUDING SPECIFICALLY (BUT NOT EXCLUSIVELY) THE DANGER OF BEING INJURED BY THROWN OR BATTED BALLS AND AGREES THAT THE PARTICIPATING CLUBS, THEIR AGENTS AND PLAYERS ARE NOT LIABLE FOR INJURIES RESULTING FROM SUCH CAUSES.

The management reserves the right to revoke the license granted by this ticket.

An example—after

The revision

- uses a contrasting typeface for the heading
- uses left-aligned headings
- uses a serifed font
- uses boldface for emphasis
- uses horizontal lines to emphasize text

Disclaimer

The holder is admitted on condition, and by use of this ticket agrees, that he will not transmit or aid in transmitting any description, account, picture or reproduction of the baseball game or exhibition to which this ticket admits him. Breach of the foregoing will automatically terminate this license.

The holder assumes all risk and dangers incidental to the game of baseball including specifically (but not exclusively) the danger of being injured by thrown or batted balls and agrees that the participating clubs, their agents and players are not liable for injuries resulting from such causes.

The management reserves the right to revoke the license granted by this ticket.

It matters how your document looks. You're not using a typewriter, so take advantage of the modern wisdom in document design and create a look that invites readers in and rewards them with accessibility and readability.

CHAPTER 3

Modern Drafting Conventions

Practice consistent, reliable, modern drafting.

Using forms

Generally speaking, there are very few forms available for plain legal drafting, so most drafters must prepare plain legal documents from scratch or from a form that contains traditional legalese. Forms save time and, therefore, money, and so they are a necessity in any legal practice. But particularly for plain legal drafting, forms present some problems.

First, forms generally contain outdated and excessively formal language. This will be the plain legal drafter's first job: to revise old-fashioned language into plain English. If the form has been used in many previous transactions, it will have the weight of precedent behind it. For the plain legal drafter, this is always a concern. If you change the form, do you risk fouling up the transaction? So when using a form, it's particularly important to make the plain-English version contain the same substance as the original form. This is why the first step in any effort to revise a traditional legal form into plain English is to take careful notes about every item of substantive content in the original. For more on the process of converting a form to plain English, see Chapter 2.

Second, forms usually contain numerous drafting inconsistencies. This is to be expected, of course, because most forms are a hodgepodge cobbled together from a variety of sources, all of which probably had different authors. So the form will not speak with a consistent voice and may contain many problematic usages.

Third, forms foster an unfortunate tendency toward haste and laziness. Because it can often be quite easy to simply change the names and change the dates to produce a first draft of a new document, using a form is deceptively easy. Experienced drafters know better. You must master the form; make it your own. Get familiar with every aspect of the form document.

Some good news for plain legal drafters is that once you have begun drafting documents for a nonlegal audience, you will begin to develop a source of plain-English forms.

Once you've mastered your forms, you can rewrite them in plain English. In doing so, implement these preferred conventions of modern legal drafting.

Recitals

In traditional legal documents, the opening paragraph, which introduces the parties, is followed by a series of paragraphs that lawyers often call the "recitals." Traditional recitals typically contain a number of "whereas" paragraphs followed by a "now therefore" paragraph, like this:

> **Original recitals**
>
> Whereas, Attorney is about to undertake the performance of substantial legal services on behalf of the Personal Representative; and
>
> Whereas, the State Bar's rules of professional conduct encourage attorneys and clients to enter into fee agreements; and
>
> Whereas, the Probate Code requires that attorney fee agreements be signed by the personal representative;
>
> Now therefore, in consideration of their mutual promises stated herein, the parties hereby agree that:

For consumer-oriented documents written in plain English, recitals aren't mandatory. They can provide helpful background, and it may be user-friendly to set the stage and explain the context, but cutting them out entirely probably wouldn't hurt anything.

You can include recitals as a way to introduce the document, provide a summary of the transaction, or clarify the intentions of the parties. If you do, abandon the stilted and archaic style of "whereas" and "now therefore."

The legal-drafting expert Kenneth Adams recommends presenting the recitals in a much more simplified way. Omit "whereas" and "now therefore," and frame each recital as a separate sentence.[1] With some other plain-English revisions, the recitals might look like this:

> **Better recitals**
>
> The Attorney is about to perform substantial legal services for the Personal Representative.
>
> The State Bar's rules of professional conduct encourage attorneys and clients to have fee agreements.
>
> The Probate Code requires that attorney fee agreements be signed by the Personal Representative.
>
> Therefore, the parties agree as follows:
>
> * * *

Defined terms and definitions

I'll address two drafting conventions in this section. The first convention is what I call defined terms (the "Defined Terms"). When I say "defined terms," I mean exactly what I did in the previous sentence: I introduced a term and then made that term into a proper noun by placing it inside parentheses and quotation marks with initial capital letters. The other drafting convention I'll discuss is definitions: creating meanings for words.

Defined terms

If you are going to be a committed plain legal drafter, you should do what you can to reduce defined terms in your documents. One

1. Kenneth A. Adams, *A Manual of Style for Contract Drafting* 11-15 (ABA 2004).

way to do that is to create and use a defined term only when you will use the term several times. In my reading of transactional documents, I am surprised at how frequently I see a defined term created and then never used. Even if the defined term is actually used once or even twice, you still might consider not creating it.

When you do create defined terms, skip the archaic or fancy conventions. Often, you can simply use the term and then put it inside parentheses with an initial capital letter.

Instead of this:

> This publishing contract is entered by Jackie Griffin (hereinafter "Griffin") and Evermore Computer Publishing House, Inc. (hereinafter "ECPHI").

Do this:

> This publishing contract is entered by Jackie Griffin (Griffin) and Evermore Computer Publishing House, Inc. (ECPHI).

And speaking of "ECPHI" (how is that pronounced?), don't create awkward acronyms or sets of initials unnecessarily. Unless Evermore Computer Publishing House, Inc. always uses the initials ECPHI, you're better off defining it as "Evermore."

To take plain English even further, let's acknowledge that when you create a defined term for a person or corporation, it is acceptable to omit the parentheses and quotation marks entirely if there is only one person or entity with that name. Old-school transactional drafters may balk at this convention, but it works:

> This publishing contract is entered by Jackie Griffin and Evermore Computer Publishing House, Inc. Griffin and Evermore have agreed that Griffin will write and Evermore will publish a book aimed at the technology market. . . .

This convention is simple, and it is the way other professionals write. Ask yourself if you have ever seen a newspaper or magazine article that looks like this:

> When local teacher and author Jackie Griffin ("Griffin") wanted to publish her book on technical writing, she first tried to go with a local publisher like Evermore Computer Publishing House, Inc. ("Evermore").

No. Avoiding that awkward convention is appropriate for plain legal drafting, too.

Definitions

I have two recommendations for definitions.

First, you should never begin a consumer document with a lengthy section of definitions. This convention may be acceptable for sophisticated transactional lawyers, but it is counterproductive and off-putting to everyday readers. Sophisticated transactional drafters like Kenneth Adams, author of *A Manual of Style for Contract Drafting*, suggest that a lengthy definitions section belongs at the end of the document, not the beginning.[2]

Second, use the word *means* and almost nothing else to introduce a definition.[3] Do not use any of the following:

> "Business Day" shall mean . . .
> "Business Day" shall have the following meaning . . .
> "Business Day" will have the following meaning . . .

Instead, use this:

> "Business Day" means . . .

Words of obligation

In any kind of binding legal text—contracts, wills, trusts, rules, regulations, and statutes—you will need to impose obligations on someone. You will need to state the duties.

In traditional transactional drafting, the most common word used to impose obligations is *shall*. Although it is often used mistakenly for the future tense, or simply to give a document a musty odor, its correct use is to impose a legal duty on the actor in a sentence, like this:

The Buyer shall pay . . .

- means *the Buyer has a duty to pay*

You shall submit a completed application . . .

- means *You are required to submit a completed application*

The Lender shall provide notice . . .

- means *the Lender has a contractual obligation to provide notice*

---

2. Kenneth A. Adams, *A Manual of Style for Contract Drafting* 81 (ABA 2004).
3. Bryan A. Garner, *A Dictionary of Modern Legal Usage* 258 (2d ed., Oxford U. Press 1995).

Whether *shall* is the right word to use to impose an obligation in traditional transactional documents is an open question. But according to Joseph Kimble, who even wrote an article called *The Many Misuses of Shall*,[4] it is certainly not the right word to use in a plain-English document.

What are your other choices? You have several:

will

- When you use *will* in binding legal text, it indicates a promise to do something. In using *will*, be careful to use it only for promises and obligations.

agree to

- When you use *agree to* in binding legal text, it indicates the party's assent to the obligation. This is another way of saying that the party promises.

promise to

- When you use *promise to* in binding legal text, it indicates a promise to do something.

must

- When you use *must* in binding legal text, it imposes an obligation on the party.

For plain legal drafting, I prefer to use *agree to* or *will*. Both are short, clear, and relatively unambiguous. I generally avoid *must* for two reasons: *must* can seem bossy, and *must* could be reserved for imposing a condition, rather than a mere promise.

Once you've decided what word or phrase to use, scan the document carefully to locate and properly frame the obligations. This means deciding which party has the obligation and what the obligation entails. In doing this, you should impose all obligations in the same language. Inconsistency in the language of obligations is sloppy, confusing, and risky. For example, I routinely encounter single documents in which the obligations are imposed in a variety of ways:

Buyer agrees to . . .
Buyer shall . . .

4. Joseph Kimble, *The Many Misuses of Shall*, 3 Scribes J. of Legal Writing 61 (1992).

> Buyer further agrees to . . .
> Buyer expressly agrees to . . .
> Buyer must . . .

And so on. This is confusing and unnecessary. Pick one phrase for imposing obligations and stick with it.

Words of discretion

Just as you should be consistent in the language of obligation, you should be consistent in the language of discretion. The general and most basic word of discretion is *may*. If I say you "may" do something, this means you have the discretion to do it. Unfortunately, the word *may* also means *might*, or *possibly*. To avoid this potential ambiguity, you have three choices.

First, you could choose to create legal documents in which the possibility of something occurring is never mentioned. This is entirely feasible for many transactional documents. Instead of saying something *may* happen, and then describing the consequences, you would say *if* something happens, and then describe the consequences.

Second, you could choose to use *may*, but limit it to one meaning. When you intend to give a party to the transaction discretion, use *may*, and only *may*, using no other words to give discretion. Then, when you want to indicate a possibility, use *might*. With this approach, you must use scrupulous care to avoid ever using *may* to mean a possibility.

Third, you could choose to use a phrase in place of *may* when you intend to give an actor discretion. With this approach, you could then use *may* for possibilities, as long as you never used it for granting discretion. Possible discretionary phrases:

- has a right to
- has authority to
- has discretion to

The keys in using words of discretion are twofold: always be sure you know whether you are granting discretion or describing a possibility, and never use one word, like *may*, to mean both.

Presenting numbers

In plain legal drafting, we abandon the tradition of doubling up numerals and text. So we do not write this:

> Seller must give notice within thirty (30) days.

And we definitely do not write this:

The purchase price is FIFTY THOUSAND AND NO 100s DOLLARS ($50,000).

This is asking for trouble. Although doubling up the numerals and text may, as some have suggested, force you to double-check your figures, it also presents twice as many opportunities to make mistakes. Pick one expression of the number (probably numerals) and stick with it.

Synonym strings

In plain legal drafting, we do all we can to avoid unnecessary doublets, triplets, and synonym strings. I can't possibly list for you every synonym string used in legal drafting with a plain-English substitute. But here is a start:

Instead of this	Try this
interpreted, construed, and governed by	governed by
power and authority	power
right, title, and interest	interest
sell, convey, assign, and transfer	sell

In general, you can go through three steps when attacking legalistic synonym strings.

1. Ask yourself: Are any of the words in the string redundant? Use a dictionary. Use a legal-usage dictionary. Then delete any redundant words.
2. Now ask yourself this: Of the remaining, nonredundant words, do you need all of them? In other words, do you need all these different meanings? If you do not, delete the words whose meanings you don't need.
3. If you still have more than one word remaining, ask yourself: Is there a single word that would cover all the meanings you need? If so, use it. If not, keep the remaining string.

Here's an example of a four-word string:

Original

The holder will not transmit any *description, account, picture, or reproduction* of the baseball game.

1. Are any of these words redundant?

- Yes, *description* and *account* are redundant, or at least redundant enough that we can eliminate one of them.[5]

2. Do we need all of the following meanings: *description, picture,* and *reproduction*?
   - No. I will be bold and take the position that we do not need the word *reproduction*. For me, it is included within the meanings of *description* and *picture*.
3. Is there a single word that will cover all the meanings we need?
   - No. To me, the word *description* covers the audio, and the word *picture* covers the visual. I think we need both.

Revision

The holder will not transmit any *description or picture* of the baseball game.

Provisos

Modifying phrases and clauses tacked on with the words *provided, provided that, provided however that,* and *provided further that* are, as Bryan Garner puts it, "a reliable signal that the draft is not going well."[6] Although there are many traditional drafting phrases that you will need to cut in a plain legal document, provisos are so frequent that they merit special attention.

The problem, besides their archaic flavor and their tendency to perplex the ordinary reader, is that provisos are vague. They can create exceptions, conditions, and additions. Better to specify what you intend with a precise term rather than to rely on a vague proviso. Often, the proviso language can simply be deleted.

Before

Insured assigns to Insurer all rights and claims the Insured may have against any person or entity who may be liable for the loss or injury resulting from the occurrence above described; *provided,*

5. *See The Oxford Dictionary and Thesaurus* 12, 382 (Am. ed. 1996).

6. Bryan A. Garner, *A Dictionary of Modern Legal Usage* 710 (2d ed. Oxford Univ. Press 1995).

however, that this assignment is limited to an amount equal to the amount of benefits paid to the Insured by Insurer with respect to the loss or injury.

After

Insured assigns Insurer all rights and claims the Insured may have against any person or entity who may be liable for the loss or injury resulting from the occurrence above described. This assignment is limited to an amount equal to the amount of benefits paid to the Insured by Insurer with respect to the loss or injury.

Placing modifiers

Transactional drafters often cause confusion by their placement of modifying words and phrases. Two problems recur: premodification and postmodification.

Premodification—placing a modifier before a list

When the modifying word or phrase comes before a list of items, it is often unclear whether the modifier applies only to the first item in the list or to all items in the list:

> This policy does not cover commercial real estate and vehicles.

Would the policy cover a noncommercial vehicle? In other words, does the word *commercial* modify *vehicles*? When you place a modifier before a list, you can create this confusion. One option is to repeat the modifier:

> This policy does not cover commercial real estate and commercial vehicles.

If you intend the other meaning, you can change the order of the items in the list:

> This policy does not cover vehicles and commercial real estate.

Postmodification—placing a modifier after a list

The same problem arises when a list is followed by a modifier. Does the modifier apply to all items in the list or only to the last item?

> The agent is not responsible for any loss, diminution in value, or failure to achieve a greater profit as a result of any investment.

Does the modifying phrase "as a result of any investment" apply only to the failure to achieve a greater profit or to all three items: the loss, the diminution in value, and the failure to achieve a greater profit? The question is not as finicky and strange as it may seem. The doctrine of the last antecedent, a widely accepted canon of construction, suggests that the modifying phrase applies only to the last item in the list.

Careful legal drafters mind their lists and frame them so that the modifiers are unambiguous. Here is one way to fix the problem of postmodification:

1. The agent is not responsible for any of the following that result from any investment:

   (a) loss,
   (b) decrease in value, or
   (c) failure to make a greater profit.

Just because we're writing in plain English doesn't mean we can ignore the conventions of better drafting. For transactional documents, even those aimed at a consumer audience, we should follow the accepted, modern conventions of legal drafting.

CHAPTER 4

Organization and Signposting

Practice informative signposting, and where flow is key, connect.

Your goal is always to make your document easy to read, but it's just as important to make it easy to skim. That is, it should be just as easy to skip around in your document as it is to read it straight through. You thus acknowledge that few will read your document from beginning to end in one sitting. Once you acknowledge this, you can better organize the document to facilitate skipping and skimming.

The title of your document

Give your document a short but descriptive title. You should aim to convey descriptive and distinguishing information with the fewest number of words. That's why short, one-word titles usually won't do:

Agreement

Disclosure

These titles are too abstract; they tell the reader almost nothing about the content of the document. Yet these more descriptive titles are needlessly long:

Attorney and Executor Agreement
on Legal Representation for the Probate Estate
of Jefferson T. Gladwell, deceased

One- and Three-month Cost-of-Funds Indexed Option
Adjustable Rate Mortgage Disclosure Statement

Be descriptive but not wordy:

Agreement to Hire a Probate Attorney

As a compromise between long and short titles, a subtitle can help:

Disclosure Statement for Your Loan
One- and Three-month Cost-of-Funds Indexed Option ARM

Once you've picked a good title, put it in a larger type size. Use boldface. And consider placement: A left-aligned title will enhance the left-aligned text, especially if all the headings are on the left margin. A centered title is traditional. A right-aligned title makes it easier to see the titles when leafing through a number of documents.

Large-scale organization—the up-front summary

When you are planning and creating the large-scale organization of your document, you are choosing and ordering the major parts. In doing so, you should keep two questions in mind.

First, what is the most important information in the document? In a persuasive document, the most important information is the result you seek, with reasons. In a demand letter, the most important information is the demand. In an opinion letter, the most important information is the opinion. For transactional drafting, the most important information may not be any one of the substantive terms; rather, it may be a summary of the transaction or a statement of its purpose.

Second, where should you place the most important information? All legal writing should begin with an up-front summary of the most important information, whether it is a preview, a thesis, or a detailed outline. So the first part of your large-scale organization is the up-front summary.

This chapter treats up-front summaries in transactional documents. For a discussion of up-front summaries in analytical documents aimed at nonlawyers, see Chapter 6.

Preparing an up-front summary in a transactional document can be tricky. As Joseph Kimble noted: "When it comes to the field that we call drafting—contracts, wills, trusts, statutes, rules, and the like—the summary will not encapsulate the analysis because there is no analysis. Rather, the summary will take the form of an introduction or overview."[1] So in a transactional document, explain what the document does and why the reader should read it.

Martin Cutts, the author of the *Oxford Guide to Plain English*, says you should "organize your material in a way that helps readers to grasp the important information early and to navigate through the document easily."[2] I agree. On a recent plain-English project for a bank, I created the following three up-front summaries for transactional documents, where the originals had contained none:

> This disclosure statement explains one- and three-month COFI Option ARM loans.
>
> This document contains notices and disclosures that are part of the loan application.
>
> This agreement allows you to lock in the interest rate (and other terms) for your loan, so you can know what interest rate you'll pay, and you can avoid the risk that rates might rise. The items you lock in are called your Pricing Package.

The length of and detail in an up-front summary will vary, depending on the length of and detail in the document.

A final note on up-front summaries: Even though the summary appears first in the document, you usually cannot write it until you have done at least one draft of the entire document. Only then will you know what belongs in the summary.

Large-scale organization—ordering

After the up-front summary, you have several options in ordering the rest of the document:

- Order of importance

1. Joseph Kimble, *First Things First: The Lost Art of Summarizing*. 8 Scribes J. of Legal Writing 103, 114 (2001–2002).
2. Martin Cutts, *Oxford Guide to Plain English* 132 (Oxford Univ. Press 2004).

- Topical order
- Order by party obligations
- Order by tradition
- Chronological order

I generally recommend arranging the main parts of a document in the order of their importance. Nearly all readers pay more attention at the beginning of the document, so it makes sense to put the most important information there and then descend to the least important information.

After order of importance, I recommend trying to order by some topic, in some logical order. Choose your topics and put them in an order that makes logical sense to you. Of course, paradoxically, the best way to test whether your own order is logical is to ask someone else to assess it.

Next, consider ordering by obligation. I have on occasion recommended that my students try ordering a bilateral contract by the obligations of the parties. This means that part one of the document is a summary, part two of the document lists all the obligations of one party, and part three lists all the obligations of the other party. The remaining sections of the document follow. This approach to ordering, which is highly unconventional in traditional transactional drafting, is very reader friendly. If the parties are actually going to read the document, then they can find all their obligations in one place. Ordering by party obligation makes things easy for the reader, but it is certainly more challenging for the drafter.

Typical transactional documents are ordered based on the order of the original form—what I call ordering by tradition. This is acceptable, but a traditional order is usually writer focused, not reader focused.

Chronological order is not a common ordering convention in legal drafting.

Small-scale organization of the document

Once you have titled the document, placed your summary up front, and ordered the main parts, you should connect those parts with small-scale organization techniques. I think of small-scale organization as having three main components:

1. Headings
2. Numbering
3. Topic and transition sentences

I discuss each here.

Headings

Headings come in two varieties. These are the first type—topic headings:

> Payment
> Arbitration
> Buyer's duties

These topic headings can be expanded into the second type of heading—explanatory headings, like these:

> Paying back your loan
> You must arbitrate disputes before suing in court
> The buyer's duties under this contract

Generally, I like to use topic headings for larger parts of the document and explanatory headings for smaller parts like subsections and paragraphs.

To make the document easy to skim, you should left align your headings, whether they are main headings, subheadings, or paragraph (inline) headings. When all the headings line up on the left margin, the document is easy to skim. The reader should still be able to determine the hierarchy of the parts of your document even without the excessive tabbing that usually indicates a hierarchy.

Relying on guidance from an expert, Bryan Garner,[3] I recommend this approach to formatting your title and headings:

Element	Description
Title	Large size, boldface, sans serif font
Main headings	Regular size, boldface, sans serif font
Subheadings	Regular size, boldface, serifed font (same font as main text)
Paragraph (inline) headings	Regular size, boldface, serifed font

3. Bryan A. Garner, *The Winning Brief: 100 Tips for Persuasive Briefing in Trial and Appellate Courts* 309 (2d ed. Oxford Univ. Press 2004).

You need not use all these levels of headings in every document, and you may pick among them for any particular document. Even in a long document, three or four levels would be enough. In practice, the document would look like this:

Title

You may or may not have text directly below the title, before the body of the document. Often you will, because this is a good place for the up-front summary or overview.

Main headings

The main headings, in a boldface, sans serif font, contrast strongly with the body text and stand out, making them easy to skim.

Subheadings

Subheadings, in the same font as the main text, stand out only because they are in boldface.

Inline heading. The inline heading, even though it is the same size as the subheading, is obviously the lowest level of the hierarchy because it is in the same line as the opening line of the text.

If the previous example had been a real document, I might have suggested to the author that it had too many headings. Just as too few headings can leave the reader swimming in a sea of undifferentiated text, too many headings can chop the document up and make it harder to skim.

Numbering

Most transactional documents should be comprehensively numbered. This means choosing a sensible numbering system and making sure that every separate provision in the document is numbered. Do not leave dangling (unnumbered) text. In addition, unlike headings, not all numbered provisions need to be left aligned—moderate tabbing can enhance readability. But whatever you do, always use hanging indentations.

Just as it is possible to have too many headings in the document, it is also possible to have too much numbering. Novices, enamored of numbering as a way to reduce imprecision, sometimes get carried away:

> **2. Monthly Bills**
>
> (A) The Attorney will bill fees, and
>
> (B) the Personal Representative will pay the fees out of the assets of the Estate monthly.
>
> (C) The Personal Representative will also pay expenses monthly.
>
> (D) Expenses include
>
> (1) copies,
>
> (2) postage,
>
> (3) long distance,
>
> (4) fax,
>
> (5) FedEx,
>
> (6) filing fees, and
>
> (7) other items.

This provision could be just as easily rendered without numbering and, because of flow, would actually be easier to read:

> **2. Monthly Bills**
>
> The Attorney will bill fees, and the Personal Representative will pay the fees out of the assets of the Estate monthly. The Personal Representative will also pay expenses monthly. Expenses include copies, postage, long distance, fax, FedEx, filing fees, and other items.

Many consumer-oriented, transactional documents are not as formal and do not need comprehensive numbering. Generally speaking, strong, skim-able headings are enough, with occasional numbering for subparts and sequential lists.

Numbering systems

Choose a sensible numbering system. For more guidance, see Chapter 2.

Topic and transition sentences

Connecting the parts and paragraphs in your document with topic and transition sentences is important for analytical legal documents like briefs, memos, and letters. It has virtually no place in legal drafting. Topics and transitions are cued with headings and numbering in transactional documents.

Other organizational aids

You can make your documents easy to read and easy to skim with two other organizational aids: a table of contents and a glossary.

Table of contents

I don't have a hard-and-fast rule, but when a single document stretches onto the fifth page, I always consider providing a table of contents near the beginning. You can use a traditional table of contents, or it can be informal, like this:

> This document has 4 parts:
>
> 1. Locking in your Pricing Package
> 2. Prepayment fees and reduced-documentation loans
> 3. Terms that apply to all options
> 4. Information about fees

Glossary

Rather than loading the front of your document with a long section of definitions, consider including a glossary at the end of the document. The glossary may include definitions for all defined terms in the document and could do double duty as an index, allowing readers to find key terms in the text.

Conclusion

Nearly all transactional documents are ordered and organized for the ease of the writer. In plain legal drafting, we focus instead on the ease of the reader. The ideal plain document uses the techniques in this chapter to make the document easy to read and easy to skim.

CHAPTER 5

Plain Letters and Email Messages

Get the point in early. Be human.

No matter your practice, you will write letters and email messages to nonlawyers at some time. In some practices, you'll do it a lot. When corresponding with nonlawyers, you must balance your desire to sound professional with your need to communicate. It's tricky, and many lawyers have swung much too far to the "sound professional" end of the spectrum. This is too bad.

Let your knowledge of the law and your ability to communicate clearly show your professionalism. Do not take the misguided approach of thinking you will impress the nonlawyer with a formal and legalistic style. Instead, when corresponding with nonlawyers, adopt a conversational tone.

But before we talk about tone, let's begin with beginnings.

Up-front summary

All communication with nonlawyers should begin with an up-front summary of some kind. It's the courteous thing to do, and it communicates much more effectively than beginning with background. The advice to begin a legal letter with an up-front summary is black-letter law; no one says different:

> By establishing the main points of a document before launching into a detailed analysis of these points, you show readers what information to look for.[1]

> I have run across [those] who thought this was the way to write reports: Feed out details gradually, "create suspense," save the big news to the last. But this is a poor way to organize a piece of writing that is chiefly information.[2]

> [K]nowing where a discussion or argument is heading is essential if a reader is to understand on first reading.[3]

> I know of only one good reason for saving big news till the end—deliberate obfuscation . . . .[4]

Yet too many letters directed at nonlawyers begin with vague background, abstractions, or—worst of all—tedious factual details such as party names and dates. This was the case with a collection letter I ran across:

> On January 31, 2005, WyTech Sales, Inc. (the "Borrower") entered into an agreement with Nuttall Systems & Technology Transfer, Inc. ("NSTT") under which all of the Borrower's accounts receivable ("Receivables") of which you are the obligor have been pledged to NSTT. The Borrower has established a lockbox (the "Lockbox") for collection of Receivables. Accordingly, you are hereby instructed to remit all payments of Receivables of which you are, or have been, the obligor to . . .

Think about how this letter begins. Frankly, the date of the agreement and even the agreement itself are background details at best and irrelevant to the reader at worst. Why not begin with an intro-

1. Frederic G. Gale & Joseph M. Moxley, *How to Write the Winning Brief* 107 (ABA 1992).
2. Robert Gunning, *The Technique of Clear Writing* 130 (McGraw-Hill 1968).
3. Lynn B. Squires, Marjorie Dick Rombauer, & Katherine See Kennedy, *Legal Writing in a Nutshell* 32–33 (2d ed., West 1996).
4. Martin Cutts, *Oxford Guide to Plain English* 134 (Oxford Univ. Press 2004).

ductory summary? Even a single sentence will do; then get to the background:

> This letter contains instructions for you to begin paying accounts you owe WyTech Sales, Inc. to Nuttall Systems & Technology Transfer, Inc.

That's the way to begin an important letter containing important instructions. Good writers begin their correspondence, whether letters or email messages, with an up-front summary on nearly every occasion. The only exceptions, truly, are personal messages and very short correspondence.

For example, all of the following openers would work well for plain-English documents; each reflects the writer's effort to communicate so as to ease the reader's way:

When giving advice or an opinion:

> You have asked if you must tell your medical patients that you receive incentives from their HMOs if you withhold certain medical services. We have concluded that although no specific law requires you to disclose the incentives, you should disclose them to avoid any possible liability.

- Notice that the opening paragraph of this letter frames the issue briefly and gives a short answer, supported by a general reason. A fuller statement of the issue with the facts, the detailed answer, and the specific reasons would follow in the body of the letter.

When making a demand:

> This firm represents First Federal Credit Union. You owe $2,250 for a signature loan and related fees. Full payment is due now.

- Resist the urge to begin a demand or settlement letter with legal or factual background. Resist the urge to build your case line by line and then place the dollar amount at the end. Accept the fact that even though you are concerned about shocking the reader by an up-front dollar amount, if you hide the dollar amount at the end of the letter, your reader will inevitably look there first anyway.

When giving instructions:

This letter outlines the four steps you will need to take to secure the mechanic's lien on the Litchfield property.

1. . . .

- Notice that summaries do not always need to contain a lot of detail. To simply preview how much information is coming may be enough. And if you tell the reader there are four things coming, why not number them?

When seeking information:

Who in your company is the appropriate person to sit for a deposition in the Anderson case? You may need some background to answer that, so here it is.

- It is a natural tendency to want to give the background before the question. That may work when you are speaking, but in writing, stating the question first allows the reader to better understand the background.

Conversational tone

After providing an up-front summary, the most important thing you can do in correspondence is adopt a conversational tone. Adopting a conversational tone does not mean writing exactly the way you speak. For most of us, our speech is far too informal, slangy, and fragmented to work well in legal correspondence. Rather, a conversational tone is one that is natural, simple, and clear. Even though it does not perfectly reflect your speech, you would be comfortable speaking the words you are writing.

For example, you should feel free to use the first- and second-person pronouns *I* and *you.* These give the message immediacy and personal appeal, and they allow you to greatly simplify the writing.

You should also feel free to use contractions when corresponding. It's fine.

But most of your efforts to use a natural and conversational tone will be directed at diction or word choice. When you have a choice between two words, one formal and one informal, your default choice should be the informal word. When you have a choice between a legal word and an everyday-English word, your default choice should be the everyday-English word. And when you have a choice between a long word and a short word, your default choice should be the short word.

Don't let your default choice override the necessity to be precise and accurate. All I'm asking you to do is abandon unnecessary legalisms, formalisms, and archaic words. Consider again the opening paragraph of our collection letter, which, by the way, was sent to a nonlawyer. Following each bracketed number, you will encounter a legalism, a tone problem, or a word-choice problem:

> On January 31, 2005, WyTech Sales, Inc. (the "Borrower") [1] entered into an agreement with Nuttall Systems & Technology Transfer, Inc. [2] ("NSTT") under which all of the Borrower's accounts receivable [3] ("Receivables") of which you are the [4] obligor have been [5] pledged to NSTT. The Borrower has established a lockbox [6] (the "Lockbox") for collection of Receivables. [7] Accordingly, you are [8] hereby instructed to [9] remit all payments of Receivables of which you are, or have been, the obligor to . . .

Let's tackle these one at a time.

1. The phrase "entered into an agreement" is, of course, a nominalization, as we will learn in Chapter 9 on sentences. We could shorten this to "agreed."
2. The initials "NSTT" are not a major problem, but it is possible to shorten the name of this entity simply to "Nuttall," isn't it? Now, if this company routinely refers to itself as "NSTT," you should use it. If not, use Nuttall.
3. To define accounts receivable as "Receivables" is not necessary unless there are other possible receivables in this letter that might cause confusion. Simply mention "accounts receivable" and from then on refer to them as "receivables" or even "accounts."
4. How many nonlawyers are going to understand the term "obligor"? Not many. We probably cannot find a one-word replacement, though. You'll see how I handle this in the rewrite.
5. Few nonlawyers are going to understand the term "pledged." Lawyers understand that this means the borrower has given Nuttall a security interest in the

receivables. Maybe we could say that. Or maybe we could say that they have been given as collateral.

6. If there is only one lockbox in this letter, you do not need to create a defined term.
7. "Accordingly" is a heavy connector, and when striving for a natural tone you should probably prefer "and" or "so."
8. Do not use archaic terms like "hereby" in a letter to a nonlawyer. Leave them out.
9. The phrase "remit all payments" is not only a nominalization, but it also contains the fancy word "remit." We can use "pay."

If you had been given this collection letter as a form document to use in preparing your own collection letter, you can see you would have needed to make extensive changes if you actually wanted it to be read and understood by a nonlawyer. Now that we have identified at least nine concerns in this letter, let's see if we can fix them:

> This letter contains instructions for you to begin paying accounts you owe WyTech Sales, Inc. to Nuttall Systems & Technology Transfer, Inc.
>
> **Background**
>
> On January 31, 2005, WyTech Sales, Inc., the borrower, gave Nuttall all its accounts receivable as collateral. You are the payer on some of these accounts. From now on, pay those accounts to a lockbox the borrower has established here: . . .

Did you notice the heading? It distinctly separates the summary from the body of the letter, allowing a busy reader to skim.

Perhaps someone reading this has expertise in collections of this sort and is screaming that I have altered the legal effect of this letter in some way. I grant that as a possibility. But I say that is a problem with my legal knowledge, not a problem with plain English or with using a conversational tone in a letter.

Even though the original tone is not particularly hostile, the tone is legalistic and formal. In reality, you would like the person receiving this letter to cooperate voluntarily and begin directing account payments to the lockbox. You are more likely to get the recipient's cooperation with a natural, nonlegal tone than you are with a formal, legalistic tone.

A final point to consider for opinion or advice letters: Most nonlegal readers will not appreciate or understand legal citations. Generally, avoid legal citations in a letter to a nonlawyer. Of course, you could cut the legal citations from the main text and paste them into footnotes, but that may add to the formality of the document, or it may distract the reader. Whatever you do, please don't do as a lawyer told me he routinely does: "I like to leave the legal citations in there because it intimidates them a little bit. When they're a little baffled, they realize they need me." If your law practice depends on intimidating and baffling your clients so they need you, good luck.

Formatting and layout

For general guidance on designing legal documents, see the advice in Chapter 2 on document design. The following is some specific guidance for letters and email.

Format letters and email messages in block-paragraph style—that is, with no tabs in the first line of each paragraph and with an extra hard return between paragraphs.

Because most letters are single-spaced, standard margins and default type sizes can make the letter look crowded. Increase the type size and push the margins in.

Don't fear headings. Any letter that fills two pages could probably benefit from headings; they allow the reader to skim and skip. You can also make the document more accessible by using numbering for sequential information and bullets for emphasizing lists.

Sending email to nonlawyers

When corresponding with nonlawyers by email, be wise. If you send a client legal advice in an email message, the client can forward the message with one click and destroy the privileged nature of the communication.

Be professional and polite. In your role as a lawyer, it's probably best to use a salutation (Dear Joan,) and a signoff (Sincerely,). But they need not be that formal. You could greet the reader informally (Joan,) and close informally too (Take care,).

Use the subject line thoughtfully. As much as possible, given the space constraints, think summary, not topic. When replying or forwarding, change the subject line as appropriate. Your readers will appreciate it.

You can't write to nonlawyers the way you write to opposing counsel or your colleagues. You've got to simplify. Your goal should be to sound natural and conversational. If this means you don't sound like a lawyer, that's great.

CHAPTER 6

Advice for Plain Court Documents

Shed hamstringing, pointless conventions. Summarize and simplify.

On occasion you may need to prepare a court document that a nonlawyer can read and understand. Granted, most legal documents are directed to a judge or opposing counsel. But if your clients actually want to read what you are doing for them, you will need to prepare a court document that is accessible to a nonlawyer.

Preparing a plain court document can be hard because the content and format of many court documents are dictated by court rules, tradition, and reliable forms. Still, I can make two helpful recommendations for simplifying court documents. One is cosmetic, and one is substantive.

Cosmetic: simplify the format and case caption

Although the appearance and format of the case caption in your court document is relatively unimportant, streamlining and simplifying it according to modern document design principles can make it more accessible to nonlawyers. Besides, it will look neat, clean, and distinctive.

Here are two typical case captions from court documents, one from federal court and one from state court.

IN THE UNITED STATES DISTRICT COURT
FOR THE EASTERN DISTRICT OF OKLAHOMA

JODY GRENDER,	)	
Plaintiff,	)	
	)	
v.	)	Civil Action No. CV-06-00985
	)	
CONSTANCE L. AMBLERTON,	)	
Commissioner,	)	
Social Security Administration,	)	
Defendant.	)	

DEFENDANT'S RESPONSE TO PLAINTIFF'S OBJECTIONS
TO COMMISSIONER'S
MOTION FOR ENTRY OF A JUDGMENT REVERSING AND
REMANDING FOR FURTHER ADMINISTRATIVE
PROCEEDINGS WITH BRIEF

NO. 07-28233-S

READY-FOODS INC.,	§	IN THE DISTRICT COURT OF
DRY-MADE, INC.	§	
Plaintiffs,	§	
	§	
v.	§	CHEROKEE COUNTY,
	§	TEXAS
	§	
SCHMIDT JONES L.L.P.,	§	
Defendant.	§	554th JUDICIAL DISTRICT

PLAINTIFFS' ORIGINAL PETITION

The truth, of course, is that there is absolutely nothing wrong with these case captions. They perform their functions well. But in an effort to modernize legal documents, here are a handful of ways to improve them.

- Eliminate the all-caps type
- Eliminate underlining
- Tighten the wording
- Tighten the spacing

If we make these changes, we have case captions that look like this:

United States District Court
Eastern District of Oklahoma

<table>
<tr><td>Jody Grender,
Plaintiff,
v.
Constance L. Amblerton,
Commissioner,
Social Security Administration,
Defendant.</td><td>)
)
)
)
)
)
)</td><td>

Civil Action No. CV-06-00985</td></tr>
</table>

Defendant's Response to Plaintiff's Objections to Commissioner's Motion for Entry of a Judgment Reversing and Remanding for Further Administrative Proceedings

No. 07-28233-S

<table>
<tr><td>Ready-Foods Inc.,
Dry-Made, Inc.
Plaintiffs,

v.

Schmidt Jones L.L.P.,
Defendant.</td><td>§
§
§
§
§
§
§
§
§</td><td>554th Judicial District

Cherokee County, Texas</td></tr>
</table>

Plaintiffs' original petition

I like these case captions. They're reader friendly and neat. They convey the same information as the originals but in a way that is shorter and more legible. Yet many lawyers resist them because they "don't look like court documents." That's only because most lawyers haven't seen enough court documents prepared by lawyers outside their community or practice area. In fact, lots of lawyers use simplified case captions like these, and they don't ruffle a feather.

Substantive: provide an up-front summary

The plain-language expert Joseph Kimble thinks every legal document should contain an up-front summary to aid the reader. In his article *First Things First: The Lost Art of Summarizing,* he says all legal writing should be front loaded and should practice the art of summarizing.[1] It's good advice that not enough lawyers follow. If you begin your court document with a boilerplate restatement of the parties and the name of the document, you can do better. Right there, at the beginning, when you have the reader's attention, get to the point.

When providing an up-front summary in a court document for a nonlawyer, you have three possible approaches.

First, you can write a full summary. The full summary contains a moderately detailed statement of the key facts, a statement of the underlying issue, and a statement of the answer—with reasons. It's appropriate for briefs and lengthy motions. It generally contains two, three, or more paragraphs, and it might look like this:

> **Full summary**
>
> The Plaintiff, Remy Gonzalez, was formerly employed as an hourly assistant manager by the corporate defendant Manor Foods, an Arby's franchisee. Gonzalez has sued both Manor Foods and one of its managers, Chris Smith, claiming that they fired Gonzalez because he has HIV, which he asserts is a disability under the Texas Commission on Human Rights Act. Through his Original Petition and First Amended Petition, he seeks lost earnings, amounts for past and future mental anguish, attorney's fees, and punitive damages. He seeks remedies only

1. Joseph Kimble, *First Things First: The Lost Art of Summarizing,* 8 Scribes J. of Legal Writing 103, 103 (2001–2002).

> under the Act, and specifically makes no claims under federal law.
>
> Manor Foods seeks a summary judgment because Gonzalez did not properly exhaust his administrative remedies as required under the Act. This court therefore lacks subject-matter jurisdiction.
>
> The individual defendant, Chris Smith, seeks dismissal of the complaint against him because he has never been Gonzalez's employer. The Act applies only to employers—not employee managers—so Gonzalez's claims against Smith should be dismissed.

Even though the writing is generally straightforward and clear, it does use some legal terminology: original petition, first amended petition, summary judgment, subject-matter jurisdiction. This is unavoidable. Yet the tone is otherwise accessible and direct. That the document provides such a thorough summary at all is itself a great aid to the nonlawyer.

Second, you can write a short summary. The short summary generally contains the conclusion with reasons, and it may contain an abbreviated statement of the facts. It's best for a short motion, an affidavit, or a complaint. It is generally one paragraph long, and it might look like this:

> **Short summary**
>
> The Plaintiff's claims against Manor Foods are based on the Texas Commission on Human Rights Act, but they do not invoke the court's subject matter jurisdiction because the Plaintiff did not exhaust his administrative remedies under the Act. Summary judgment is therefore proper. The Plaintiff's claims against Chris Smith are also based on the Act. But Smith was never the Plaintiff's employer under the Act, so the Act does not apply. The Plaintiff's claims against Smith should therefore be dismissed.

The short summary leaves out some details and does not spell out the legal argument fully. That's okay. It gets the key points across, and that's what's important.

Third, you can use a single-sentence summary—what I also call the preview summary. It does little more than preview the content. It usually does not contain any facts or even a conclusion.

Rather, it simply gives a brief introduction to the content. It's best for a short affidavit or for a sub-part or section of a larger document. It might look like this:

> **Single-sentence (preview) summary**
>
> This court should grant Manor Foods a summary judgment against the Plaintiff and should dismiss the Plaintiff's claims against Chris Smith.

Every court document should use some kind of up-front summary. Gauge your document's length and complexity, and choose your approach.

The summary works in all court documents—everywhere

Far too many court documents, whether intended for legal readers or nonlegal readers, begin poorly. They begin with general background, with a series of dates, or with the worst possible opener of all:

> COMES NOW Defendant Kit Rail Transport (Kit), by and through its attorney of record, and files this, its Motion to Dismiss for Failure to State a Claim Upon Which Relief Can be Granted, and in support thereof would respectfully show unto the court as follows:

This form of opener has been rightly criticized by many:

> By devoting the entire opening paragraph to restating the needlessly long title, lawyers waste judges' time and sacrifice a valuable chance for persuasion.[2]
>
> If you begin a brief noncommittally with, "This is a brief in opposition to defendant's motion for summary judgment," you may be avoiding the challenge of determining your best fact and building a theme around it. At the very least, you are forfeiting the opportunity to use the premier sentence in your brief—the opening sentence—for persuasive purposes.[3]

---

2. Beverly Ray Burlingame, *On Beginning a Court Paper,* 6 Scribes Journal of Legal Writing 160, 161 (1997).

3. Kenneth F. Oettle, *Making Your Point: A Practical Guide to Persuasive Legal Writing 9* (ALM 2007).

> Do you begin your court papers by introducing the parties and the procedural background? Stop it. You're squandering a great chance to get your point across.[4]

> Formulaic phrases are easy to adopt. . . . Perhaps this is how litigators got into the habit of wasting their openers by repeating—more or less verbatim—the very words of the title.[5]

Still, the practice is surprisingly common and unfortunate. I'm here to tell you that you can use an up-front summary in nearly every court document you prepare. I have already offered examples from a brief and a motion, so below I offer examples for a complaint and an affidavit.

Up-front summary for a complaint

> This is an action seeking a declaratory judgment that a rule issued by the Idaho Alcohol Beverage Control agency is unconstitutional.

This kind of summary is unusual in complaints. Generally speaking, complaints begin with a formulaic restatement of the title or with a numbered section stating the parties, the jurisdiction, or some other aspect of the procedural background. But the advice to begin a complaint with a brief summary of the nature of the case was offered as far back as 1987 by Irwin Alterman in his book *Plain and Accurate Style in Court Papers.* He recommends opening with a paragraph describing the nature of the action even before you introduce and identify the parties.[6]

Alterman's book is now 20 years old, but his advice is as helpful today as ever. Whether you must show your court documents to your nonlawyer clients or not, the up-front summary approach will help you improve the way you prepare them.

Now for a more controversial recommendation—for affidavits.

Up-front summary for an affidavit

> In this affidavit, Randall Colton, district manager for CarZone, Inc., states that it has been and is company policy

---

4. Wayne Schiess, *Writing for the Legal Audience* (Carolina Academic Press 2003).

5. Bryan A. Garner, *The Winning Brief: 100 Tips for Persuasive Briefing in Trial and Appellate Courts* 344 (2d ed., Oxford U. Press 2004).

6. Irwin Alterman, *Plain and Accurate Style in Court Papers* 38 (ALI-ABA 1987).

> to reprimand an employee after a first-time no-show for a scheduled shift. He also states that it has been and is company policy to demote an employee on the second no-show for a scheduled shift.

Granted, it is unusual to provide an up-front summary for an affidavit. An affidavit is a written form of testimony and, generally speaking, we do not provide an up-front summary when we speak. But an affidavit is a written document, and providing an up-front summary will greatly aid the reader.

So you won't think I'm completely out in left field, here is a testimonial from a lawyer who has begun to use an up-front summary in affidavits:

> I was finally able to use the suggestions about affidavits. . . . The senior partner I'm working with immediately adopted this for the affidavits he wrote and said he's going to add the up-front summary to every affidavit he does "for the rest of my life."

Whether it is unusual to use an up-front summary in an affidavit—or in a complaint, motion, or brief, for that matter—ought to be a secondary concern. The primary concern is whether a nonlawyer who must read and understand the document can do so. A clearly written up-front summary will help.

Streamline the look of your court documents. Bring them into the 21st century. Summarize right up front. Get to the point. You'll do more than aid the nonlegal reader—you'll begin to persuade the judge.

CHAPTER 7

Testing Your Plain Drafts

Try several testing techniques. Seek critiques. Accept them.

Once you have completed your plain legal document, you should test it on nonlawyers—the intended audience. No matter how carefully you write, and no matter what readability scales you use, there is no substitute for feedback from the reader. Sophisticated testing is not always feasible, and you may not always have a lot of time. But whenever possible, do at least some testing.

Benefits of testing

Most writers are not comfortable with critique. It's difficult to accept comments and criticism. It's difficult to acknowledge that what seems clear to us is a muddle to someone else. But in my experience, testing always improves the text.

Testing helps you uncover mistakes. As embarrassing as it is to have testers tell you that you misspelled a word or left out a comma, it is far less embarrassing than having the mistake survive into the final document.

Testing allows you to get a true gauge of the audience's preferences. Most of the time, when preparing a plain legal document, you are making assumptions about what the reader needs, how the reader will use the document, and what the reader already knows. When you test your document on the intended audience, you get facts.

For example, I distinctly remember watching live mock-jury deliberations and realizing that the jurors were misunderstanding the word *unanimous*. I had taken it for granted that everyone would know what *unanimous* means. Not so. In the context of certain jury instructions, some questions could be agreed upon by only 10 of the 12 jurors. In our situation, the next instruction said, "If you were unanimous on question 2, then answer question 3." The jurors mistakenly believed that if the same 10 people agreed on question 3 as had agreed on question 2, that was unanimous. Having learned of this confusion, we immediately revised the draft instructions: "If all 12 of you agreed on question 2, then answer question 3."

Testing also produces empirical evidence to support the effectiveness of plain English. For example, it might have been difficult to persuade a pattern jury charges oversight committee that typical jurors do not understand the word *unanimous*. But because we did testing, we had videotaped evidence. And we had videotapes showing jurors deliberating with our new instructions, which excluded the word *unanimous*. With the new instructions, there was no confusion.

Testing methods

Here I'll describe several plain-language testing methods I have used. For further information on testing, consult these sources:

- Chapter 17 in *Plain Language for Lawyers* by Michele M. Asprey
- Chapter 5 in *A Plain Language Handbook for Legal Writers* by Christine Mowat

Informal testing

Sometimes you can just ask someone about a piece of writing on the spot, orally. "Here. Read this. What do you think?" The more specific the question, the more it may come off like an interrogation, but the better the feedback is likely to be. You can move from broad (what do you think?) to moderately specific (do you understand this paragraph?) to narrowly specific (what does this sentence or word mean?).

One of my favorite testing techniques is to send an email message to a group of my friends and solicit their input on a piece of legal writing. Usually, since it is in writing, I am able to ask narrower questions and get better feedback.

An easy approach is to send before-and-after versions (not labeled) and ask which they prefer. I have also sent a piece of text and asked recipients to explain what it means in their own words. And I've asked recipients to read a piece of text and answer multiple-choice questions about it. In reality you're giving them a test, but surprisingly, if you tell them it's to improve legal writing, they'll usually be glad to help.

Another informal way to test a piece of plain legal writing is to ask a nonlawyer to read and critique it. I have used this technique effectively on a few occasions.

Sometimes you must persuade readers that you sincerely want their candid reactions. Often, those without legal training assume that if they do not understand something or if the writing seems dense it's because they aren't lawyers. Usually, if you explain your goals and genuinely accept their feedback, you'll be able to persuade them that the reactions of a typical nonlawyer are precisely what you're looking for.

Informal testing has drawbacks. Because it is informal, your results may not be statistically valid. So informal testing generally produces only anecdotal support rather than solid evidence. Yet this is often enough for making edits and revisions.

Formal testing

You can use many of the same testing methods mentioned above in more formal settings. Generally, this means that the test takers are not acquainted with you, are selected randomly, and are verifiably representative of the document's intended audience.

Once you have a group of test takers, you can ask them to read and compare before-and-after versions of the text. You should guide their comparisons with clear instructions and probably with specific questions. You can also ask one group of test takers to read the original and answer questions, and then ask another group to read the revision and answer the same questions. If the educational backgrounds of the two groups are relatively similar, you can compare the results.

I participated in a two-day test of pattern jury charges that was handled this way. On day one, 48 mock jurors in four groups of 12 deliberated on a mock case using the original pattern jury charges. They then answered a series of true/false and multiple-choice questions. On day two, 48 different mock jurors repeated the process using the revised jury charges. Because the educational and demographic makeup of the two groups was similar, we validly compared the results of the tests. Incidentally, by modest margins, the revised jury instructions scored better than the original.

If you have the time and the patience, one of the best kinds of formal testing to use on a plain legal document is a read-and-apply test. Again, you use two groups of test takers. The first group reads the original legal text and then uses it to solve a problem, fill out a form, or answer a legal question. A second group completes the same exercises using the revised text. Professor Joseph Kimble has used this approach on groups of legal secretaries and law students with excellent results.[1]

Formal testing has drawbacks, too. Mainly, it's expensive. In our jury charge testing, we hired a pricey jury consultant who in turn hired an actor to play the judge and paid a modest *per diem* to the mock jurors. These expenses added up. What's more, it is often time-consuming, and it can be difficult to create valid test questions.

To genuinely improve your plain legal drafts, you must test. Even the most experienced experts at legal drafting recognize this. Honest critique will improve the writing and expose problems you weren't aware of.

1. Joseph Kimble, *Answering the Critics of Plain Language,* 5 Scribes Journal of Legal Writing 51, 69–71 (1994–1995).

CHAPTER 8

Words

Nix foreign and archaic words, legal jargon, and dispensable terms of art. Explain indispensable legal words. Favor the crisp, the natural, and the personal.

This chapter covers the most controversial aspect in all of plain legal writing: words. For the most part, words are what make legal language sound legal. More than our documents, more than our paragraphs, and more than our sentences, our words set us apart as lawyers. Simplify the words, and the text sounds like regular English. So when I tell lawyers to change their words—to simplify them—I am almost telling them to change their identities. That's a problem for some lawyers.

Lawyers are smart and often well read. We're used to reading and using tough vocabulary. We're capable of handling the big words and the legal terminology, so some of us wonder why we should simplify. We've worked hard to master the specialized language we call legal English, and we don't want to limit ourselves.

But let's be clear: to write plainly you do not need to limit your own vocabulary or your own understanding of words. In fact, the larger your vocabulary, the better of a writer you are likely to be.

As Rudolf Flesch said, you just have to use the right words at the right times and places:

> So if you have a big vocabulary and know a lot of rare and fancy words, that's fine. Be proud of your knowledge. It's important in reading and in learning. But when it comes to *using* your vocabulary, don't throw those big words around where they don't belong. They are handy for writing formal letters and essays or for scientific and scholarly discussions. Also for solving crossword puzzles. But they're not good for informal use. . . .
>
> So it's a good rule to know as many rare words as possible for your reading, but to use as few of them as possible in your writing.[1]

In this chapter, I'll first introduce five types of words that aren't right for plain legal drafting: Latin and French, archaic words, legalese and jargon, terms of art, and hyperformal words. Then I'll suggest some words that will make your text crisp, natural, and personal.

Latin and French

Generally speaking, you should do everything you can to avoid using Latin and French in documents for nonlawyers. If you're preparing a document for an audience of lawyers, that's a different matter. You might still choose to avoid unnecessary Latin and French, and I think that's wise. But in a document for nonlawyers, you should never use a word like the French *cestui que trust* or words like the Latin *sua sponte* or *inter alia*. Even unavoidable Latin terms of art like *habeas corpus* should be used only as a last resort and must be defined when used.

Archaic words

Avoid obviously archaic terms. They have no place in drafting for nonlawyers. In every case there are plain-English equivalents. For example, in a contract for representation of a professional athlete, I found all of these archaic words:

hereof
hereto
hereunder

1. Rudolf Flesch, *How to Write Better* 25, 35 (Science Res. Assocs., Inc. 1951).

hereinafter
in witness whereof
thereafter
thereof
thereon
witnesseth

These words make the contract, which was signed in 2004, sound as if it were written in 1804.

In the case of archaic words beginning with "here" and "there," you have simple substitutes available. Here is a before-and-after version of a paragraph from the same contract with the archaic terms highlighted:

Before—with archaic words

Player also shall reimburse Contract Advisor for all reasonable and necessary travel expenses actually incurred by Contract Advisor during the term **hereof** in the negotiation of Player's NFL contract, but only if such expenses and approximate amounts **thereof** shall be approved in advance by Player.

After—with everyday English

Player also shall reimburse Contract Advisor for all reasonable and necessary travel expenses actually incurred by Contract Advisor during the term **of this agreement** in the negotiation of Player's NFL contract, but only if such expenses and approximate amounts **of those expenses** shall be approved in advance by Player.

Yes, the everyday English version takes more words than the archaic version. That is a natural and sometimes unavoidable consequence of converting a legal document into language a nonlawyer can read and understand. Don't worry; in nearly every document, you will more than make up for the excess words by shortening other provisions.

The archaic words from this contract aren't the only archaic words worth eliminating. There are lots more. Some others are

aforesaid
be it remembered
comes now
foregoing

further affiant sayeth not
know all men by these presents
said (adjective)
same (noun)
therefor
to wit
undersigned
whereas
wherefore, premises considered

If you encounter a word that's not listed here, how do you know if it's archaic? You can trust your common sense, or you can look the word up in a dictionary, legal dictionary, or legal-usage dictionary. For guidance on all things related to legal words, I recommend two sources:

- *A Dictionary of Modern Legal Usage*, by Bryan A. Garner
- *Mellinkoff's Dictionary of American Legal Usage*, by David Mellinkoff

Legalese and jargon

Train yourself to spot and revise words and phrases that only lawyers use. Consider them insider language, not appropriate for nonlawyers. A comprehensive list of legal words and insider jargon could fill this chapter, but here is a short list to get you started:

action
agent
case at bar
consideration
duly
execute (for *sign*)
fee simple
holding
instant case
intestate
pursuant to

One simple test for legalese and jargon is to ask yourself whether a nonlawyer would give the word the same meaning you do. Take *action*, for example. To you, it's a lawsuit. To a nonlawyer, it's the process of doing. So when you write that clients can "bring an action against" someone, you're using legalese. Instead, write that they can "sue" someone. *Sue* may be a legal term, but it's one every-one knows. We are not striving to eliminate all legal words, just the ones only lawyers use.

Terms of art

The law has terms of art. No one disputes this. Where plain-English advocates and typical lawyers disagree is on the number of terms of art. Some lawyers see them everywhere. But those who have studied the question, as Joseph Kimble has, assert that real terms of art are rare in the law: "True terms of art, technical terms with a fairly precise meaning, are far less common than lawyers tend to think."[2]

For example, court decisions do not always terms of art make. Many lawyers assume that when a court has issued an opinion that explains or defines a term, it becomes a term of art. But don't forget that the case law supporting the definitions of terms of art is constantly evolving. Mellinkoff said this 25 years ago: "You can't rely on precedent alone to make a term of art. . . . There is too much of it. And it keeps changing."[3] So be stingy in labeling a word a term of art.

Even if you've got a legitimate term of art, if you can cut it, do. Don't use a complex legal word in your document and simply fall back on the excuse that it is a term of art. Look it up. Consult a legal dictionary, a legal-usage dictionary, or *Words and Phrases.* Ask someone.

But sometimes using a term of art is unavoidable. I once redrafted a notice about interest-rate changes for a credit-card agreement. I changed the phrase "our then-current rate" to "the interest rate we're using when you apply." An industry lawyer who was reviewing the draft suggested we retain "current" because in the industry, it meant "within 30 days." Fine.

Another option is to use the term of art and then give a short, everyday English explanation. Here's an example from our professional sports contract (the term of art is *fiduciary capacity*):

Before

In performing these services, Contract Advisor acknowledges that he/she is acting in a **fiduciary capacity** on behalf

2. Joseph Kimble, *Lifting the Fog of Legalese* 113 (Carolina Academic Press 2006).

3. David Mellinkoff, *Legal Writing: Sense and Nonsense* 8 (West 1982).

> of Player and agrees to act in such manner as to protect the best interests of Player and assure effective representation of Player in individual contract negotiations . . .
>
> **After**
>
> In performing these services, Contract Advisor acknowledges that he or she is acting in a **fiduciary capacity—meaning with the utmost good faith**—on behalf of Player and agrees to act in such manner as to protect the best interests of Player and assure effective representation of Player in individual contract negotiations . . .

Here is another example of an indispensable term of art, *privilege,* found in a jury instruction:

> You are instructed that you may not draw an adverse inference from the witness's claim of **privilege**.

I was the drafting consultant on the task force charged with redrafting this instruction. We all agreed that *privilege* was a legal term of art and that we ought to keep it. It has a relatively well-settled meaning in the law. But we also agreed that most nonlawyers would not know what it meant. So we retained the word *privilege* but defined it for the nonlegal reader:

> **A privilege is the right not to testify.** You are instructed that you may not draw an adverse inference from the witness's claim of **privilege**.

I will have more to say about this "privilege" jury instruction in the next section.

Hyperformality

The urge to sound serious and educated drives a lot of dense legal writing. But hyperformality also arises from the use of outdated forms and from the misguided desire to intimidate or baffle the nonlegal reader. Shed that attitude; strive to communicate, not to impress.

Hyperformality causes lawyers to use all the problematic kinds of words we've just discussed: Latin, French, archaic words, insider legal jargon, and unnecessary terms of art. But these are only a small part of any legal text. What about all the other words? Even there, we can do more.

I want you to consider eliminating—here I go, opening myself up to savage criticism—"big words." Before I launch into a diatribe against big words, I want to remind you that it is not my goal to dumb down your vocabulary. It is not my goal to force all legal writing to a fourth-grade level. Rather, I am focused on communicating legal concepts to nonlawyers. To do that, and to do it effectively, we need to bring our writing to their level.

I could give you a list of big words with their everyday English equivalents, but someone else has already done that. Joseph Kimble, the legal-writing expert, has published two articles that contain lists of big words and phrases with a parallel list of everyday English:

- Joseph Kimble, *Plain Words (Part 1)*, 80 Mich. B.J. 72 (Aug. 2001).
- Joseph Kimble, *Plain Words (Part 2)*, 80 Mich. B.J. 72 (Sept. 2001).

Go look at his lists (I'm sure you'll agree I'm rather tame in my goals compared to Professor Kimble) and get all the venting about dumbing down out of your system.

Done?

Now you can put the lists aside. I want you to use your intuition. Steep yourself in the world of plain English, then put yourself inside the heads of your nonlegal readers. Figure out what words they are likely to know. Think about a time you did some reading in another field. When you're reading something unfamiliar, the simpler the words, the better, right?

We can all get inside the heads of our nonlegal readers. Here's a story offering evidence that nearly all lawyers, when they are motivated, are well aware of the kinds of words that ordinary readers will not understand.

I have served as the drafting consultant to a task force revising a portion of the Texas pattern jury charges into plain English. As a member of the task force, I had occasion to attend a meeting of the pattern jury charges oversight committee. This committee reads and approves all changes to the pattern jury charges. At the meeting I attended, there were about 12 members of the oversight committee present. The committee members were judges and lawyers from around the state.

At one point in the meeting, we were discussing a jury charge our task force had not yet revised. It was the charge quoted earlier, telling the jury what to do when a witness exercised a privilege:

> You are instructed that you may not draw an adverse inference from the witness's claim of privilege.

When this language was read out loud and was put on the projection screen, there was an immediate consensus—in fact there was unanimity—that nonlawyers would not understand certain words in the instruction.

What particular words in this charge (besides "privilege") do you think the members of the oversight committee realized would be hard for ordinary jurors?

It's obvious, isn't it? The words were "draw an adverse inference." No one had to look it up. No one had to consult a usage dictionary. No one had to conduct a poll of nonlegal readers. All of us knew, instinctively, that these words were too fancy, too formal—too big.

Specifically, *draw* as used in this phrase means "to conclude" and not "to sketch." As we've seen, it's fairly common for an everyday English word to have an unconventional meaning when used by a lawyer. Next, *adverse* is just a fancy way of saying *bad*. And *inference* is problematic, too. Even laywers get confused about *infer* and its forms.

You can recognize problematic words, just as we could. You simply have to tune your ear and mind to the level of the ordinary reader. By the way, once we decided that jurors should not draw even positive inferences from the witness's claim of privilege, we proposed this revision to the oversight committee:

> A privilege is the right not to testify. Do not assume anything when a witness uses a privilege.

Crisp, natural, personal

For legal documents that must be read and understood by nonlawyers, you want the text to be crisp. You want it to be natural—what I sometimes call "alive"—and, if possible, you want it to be personal. That way, readers feel that the document is speaking *to* them—not *at* them. Some great techniques for making your writing crisp, natural, and personal are to avoid complex prepositions, nominalizations, the passive voice, and excessive modifiers. All these topics are discussed in Chapter 9.

But in my experience revising traditional legal language into plain English, the single most effective technique for making a document crisp, natural, and personal is the use of the personal pronouns *you, I, we,* and *us.* This is not a new idea. The language expert Rudolf Flesch was recommending this technique in the 1970s. He considered what he called "the *you* style" to be indispensable for plain English.

Two examples should make the point.

Imagine that your parent has died and that you have been named the administrator or personal representative of the estate. You have decided to hire a lawyer to help you handle the matter. The lawyer hands you an "hourly fee agreement" that contains the following language (oh—and pretend you are not a lawyer):

> Attorney is about to undertake the performance of substantial legal services on behalf of the Personal Representative, for which Attorney shall be paid fees and costs. The Personal Representative has retained Attorney to provide legal services to the Personal Representative for administration of the probate estate.

I hope you'll agree that this text has several problems. But we can improve it tremendously, and make it seem more immediate to the reader, if we simply use the words *you* and *me*:

> I am about to undertake the performance of substantial legal services on behalf of you, for which I shall be paid fees and costs. You have retained me to provide legal services to you for administration of the probate estate.

Now, some might object that the original words *attorney* and *personal representative* were probably defined somewhere earlier in the document and consistency requires us to use them throughout. But we could likewise define *you* and *I* earlier in the document and use them throughout.

Here is another example that highlights two other benefits of the *you* approach. When you use awkward initials and when you insist on working around personal pronouns, you sound like a machine. You can avoid both those practices with the *you* approach.

Original

> Therapeutic Recovery Care Hospital for Children ("TRCHC") has provided this web site for educational and informational

> purposes only. The material contained herein is believed to be complete and generally in accord with accepted standards at the time of publication. However, because of the possibility of human error and changes in medical science, TRCHC and its employees do not warrant that the information contained herein is in every respect accurate or complete, and thus, are not responsible for any errors or omissions or for the results obtained from the use of such information. TRCHC makes no representation or warranties, expressed or implied, and disclaims any liability for injury and any other damages which result from an individual using techniques discussed on this site.

The stiff and impersonal tone, as well as the hard-to-pronounce initials, are largely the result of avoiding personal pronouns. Besides, we can spot several archaic legal words and some hyperformality, can't we? Let's fix it all:

Original	Revision
Therapeutic Recovery Care Hospital for Children ("TRCHC") has provided this web site for educational and informational purposes only.	We (the Therapeutic Recovery Care Hospital for Children and its employees) provide this website for education and information only.
The material contained herein is believed to be complete and generally in accord with accepted standards at the time of publication.	We believe the material here is complete and that it generally met accepted standards when we published it.
However, because of the possibility of human error and changes in medical science, TRCHC and its employees do not warrant that the information contained herein is in every respect accurate or complete, and thus, are not responsible for any errors or omissions or for the results obtained from the use of such information.	But because people make mistakes and medical science changes, we don't warrant that the information is entirely accurate or complete. We aren't responsible for any errors or omissions or for the results if you use this information.

TRCHC makes no representation or warranties, expressed or implied, and disclaims any liability for injury and any other damages which result from an individual using techniques discussed on this site.

We make no representations or warranties, expressed or implied, and we're not liable for injury and any other damages if you use techniques discussed on this site.

Revised

We (the Therapeutic Recovery Care Hospital for Children and its employees) provide this website for education and information only. We believe the material here is complete and generally met accepted standards when we published it. But because people make mistakes and medical science changes, we don't warrant that the information is entirely accurate or complete. We aren't responsible for any errors or omissions or for the results if you use this information. We make no representations or warranties, expressed or implied, and we're not liable for injury and any other damages if you use techniques discussed on this site.

I can boil this chapter down to this advice: think of your reader. If you do, you'll banish foreign and archaic words. You'll never write for nonlawyers as if they were legal insiders. And you'll speak directly to your reader with *you* and with everyday words whenever you can.

CHAPTER 9

Sentences

Manage sentence length. Use an actor. Punctuate for precision, and cut, cut, cut.

Control your sentence length

When you are drafting legal text for a nonlegal audience, what is the longest any single sentence should be? And what is a good average sentence length? Countless legal writing experts have discussed these questions, and many have offered recommendations. Let me tell you what I think.

Let's begin with sentence length. Why do legal sentences often end up so long? Perhaps it's because of the cases we read in law school. Long sentences abound in judicial opinions. In fact, that influence is so strong on students that many years ago I began to track the longest sentences in student papers. For a number of years, the record for the longest sentence was 97 words. But just a few years ago that record was shattered by a student-written sentence of 114 words. Of course, that is an aberration. But it is perhaps indicative of the overall problem lawyers have with long sentences.

Perhaps we write long sentences, particularly in transactional documents, because we believe in what Howard Darmstadter calls a myth—that an idea and all its qualifications must be contained in a single sentence:

> When a general statement is subject to an exception or two, why do drafters feel that the exceptions must be

> packed into the same sentence as the general statement? For many drafters, the unit of truth is the sentence. . . . [E]ach sentence must be true taken by itself—that is, its truth or falsity cannot be allowed to depend on some other sentence or sentences. . . . Such a position is, of course, ridiculous.[1]

In their excellent book, *Clear Understandings*, Goldfarb and Raymond debunk the single-sentence myth as well:

> [Lawyers] think that in order to achieve clear understandings, they must stuff every related idea into a single sentence between an initial capital letter and a final period. They are, of course, wrong.[2]

So use multiple sentences. And watch your maximum sentence length.

Maximum sentence length

Any single sentence that is longer than 45 words will probably challenge a nonlawyer. In fact, depending on the complexity of the sentence structure and the density of the subject matter, even a much shorter sentence can be a challenge. The goal is not to challenge the reader, but to inform and communicate.

Of course, if the sentence is well constructed, especially if it contains elegant, parallel phrases in a series, it can be much longer than 45 words and still be understandable. So my recommendation of 45 words as a maximum sentence length is just that, a recommendation.

If you agree with me that you must watch your maximum sentence length, be practical about it. You don't count the number of words in your sentences as you write. Controlling sentence length occurs primarily during the edit. If, in reading a single sentence, I find myself growing weary or bogging down, I highlight the sentence, click "word count," and assess the length. (I usually edit on a computer screen, and I have a button for Word Count on my toolbar.) If the length is over 45 words, I revise.

---

1. Howard Darmstadter, *Hereof, Thereof, and Everywhereof: A Contrarian Guide to Legal Drafting* 41 (ABA 2002).
2. Ronald L. Goldfarb & James C. Raymond, *Clear Understandings: A Guide to Legal Writing* 47 (West 1982).

Average sentence length

When I ask lawyers about average sentence length in a public setting, such as one of my seminars, I get a variety of answers. For example, I have had a lawyer suggest that 35 words per sentence is a good average. That's too long, I think. But I have also had a lawyer suggest that 8 words per sentence is a good average. That's not realistic, I think. Generally speaking, in a legal text aimed at nonlegal readers, if the text does not contain citations, the average sentence length should be 20 words per sentence or fewer.

But you don't have to take my word for it. Here are recommended average sentence lengths from the experts:

- Below 25, says Richard Wydick in *Plain English for Lawyers.*
- About 22, say Anne Enquist and Laurel Currie Oates in *Just Writing: Grammar, Punctuation, and Style for the Legal Writer.*
- About 20, says Bryan A. Garner in *Legal Writing in Plain English.*

And when you write about complex subjects, push the average length down. In *Writing to Win,* litigator and teacher Steven Stark says that the more complicated your information is, the shorter your sentences should be.[3]

I am practical about average sentence length, too. I do not assess it until I am editing the text. I have programmed my spell checker to give me statistical information about my document each time I spell check. If my average sentence length is in the teens, I am usually satisfied. If it is over 20, I may search for and revise the longest sentences. Note: if the text has short headings and lots of tabulation, these will drive the average sentence length down.

Finally, when I suggest an average sentence length, I do not mean to imply that all sentences should be of that length. Rather, you should vary your sentence length appropriately to avoid a choppy writing style.

Beyond sentence length, you can do a number of things to write readable sentences.

Replace nominalizations

A "nominalization" is a verb that has been turned into a noun. When I say "make a payment" in place of "pay," I am using a nominalization. Nominalizations abound in legal writing:

3. Steven D. Stark, *Writing to Win: The Legal Writer* 33 (Main Street Books 1999).

Nominalized form	**Verb form**
your attendance is required	you must attend
bring suit against	sue
make an application	apply
interpose an objection	object
have knowledge of	know
reach an agreement	agree

When you use a nominalization, you must add extra words to get the same meaning. When you use a lot of nominalizations, you need a lot of extra words, and you usually end up putting your reader to sleep.

Nominalizations are a classic hallmark of traditional legalese. So one way to control your sentence length, avoid legalese, and make your sentences speak to the reader is to replace nominalizations.

In this excerpt from a law-firm website disclaimer, the nominalizations are highlighted:

With nominalizations

Reproduction of all or part of the contents of this page in any form is prohibited other than for individual use and it may not be recopied and shared with a third party. The **permission** to recopy by an individual does not allow for **incorporation** of this material or any part of it in any work or publication, whether in hard copy, electronic, or any other form.

With verbs instead

You may not **reproduce** all or part of the contents of this page in any form—other than for individual use, and you may not recopy and share it with a third party. If we **permit** you to recopy, you may not **incorporate** this material or any part of it into any work or publication, whether in hard copy, electronic, or any other form.

The revised text is only four words shorter, but it is more alive. In other words, it is beginning to speak to the reader, instead of droning on in dull legalese. So when you edit, look for nouns, especially big nouns, that could be verbs. One hint is that many nominalizations end in "-ion." Then replace the nouns with the verb form.

Practice consistent parallelism

Express related ideas in parallel form. This is fairly easy to say, but the trick is to do it consistently, without fail. Your reward will be text that is easy to read and understand. In fact, to the extent you write in perfectly parallel form, you have freedom to create longer sentences. The so-called "periodic sentence," which contains a lead-in and a series of parallel phrases or clauses, is probably the only way to create long sentences that are easy to read.

Drafting for the nonlegal audience presents many opportunities for parallelism. My standards for parallelism require that all the items or phrases in the series can fit directly with the lead-in and that all the items or phrases in the series begin with the same part of speech. To test for parallelism, tabulate the items or phrases in the series (put each on its own line), even if you will not tabulate them in the final document. For example:

Original—not parallel

Publisher has the right to determine (1) the number of copies to be printed, (2) the method and style of the print and binding, (3) how to advertise and sell the book, (4) publish the book in one or more volumes and in any style it thinks is best suited to its sale, and (5) set the price of the book.

The easiest way to see that the original is not parallel is to tabulate it; that is, to place each numbered item on its own line:

Nonparallel original—as tabulated

Publisher has the right to determine

1. the number of copies to be printed,
2. the method and style of the print and binding,
3. how to advertise and sell the book,
4. publish the book in one or more volumes and in any style it thinks is best suited to its sale, and
5. set the price of the book.

Now we can see that the individual items do not all fit with the lead-in "determine." What's more, the numbered items do not begin with the same part of speech. How does this happen? Generally, when the phrases in a series are presented in a paragraph format rather than a tabulated format, the writer can sometimes lose track of the lead-in. And the longer the list of phrases, the more likely it is that the drafter will forget how each phrase is to begin.

For ease of reading, be scrupulous in applying strict parallelism.

Parallel revision

Publisher has the right

1. to determine the number of copies to be printed,
2. to determine the method and style of the print and binding,
3. to determine how to advertise and sell the book,
4. to publish the book in one or more volumes and in any style it thinks is best suited to its sale, and
5. to set the price of the book.

Find "actors" for your sentences and put them to work

Plain-English legal drafting requires you to constantly consider this question: Who is doing the action in this sentence? Who is the "actor"? By focusing on this question, you make the text more immediate, alive, and readable. And you avoid some common pitfalls.

To fully discuss the use of actors in our sentences, we must understand the passive voice. A passive-voice construction exists when you use a form of the verb *be* (be, am, is, are, was, were, being, been) followed by a past participle (the form of a verb that fits here: have _____, as in *have walked* and *have written*). Thus, the following are passive voice constructions:

- If the market price is increased to $8,000 . . .
- After the notices are received . . .
- The full purchase price shall be paid . . .

Each contains a form of the verb *be* and a past participle:

- is + [have] increased
- are + [have] received
- be + [have] paid

Please also notice that there is no actor in any of these examples. This is the primary drawback of the passive voice in transactional drafting: the absence of an actor.

The key to revising passive voice constructions in legal drafting is to identify the appropriate actor—acknowledging that in some circumstances it may be okay to leave the actor unidentified.

In the following sentence, for example, the absence of an actor is entirely appropriate:

- If the market price is increased to $8,000, . . .

In this sentence, who is the actor? In other words, who is it that is increasing the purchase price? In fact, it is no one. There are many circumstances in transactional drafting in which an action simply occurs and it is entirely appropriate to state it without identifying an actor. Still, we could improve this text by eliminating the passive voice and converting to present tense, active voice:

- If the market price increases to $8,000, . . .

But most of the time, we would do well to identify an actor as we eliminate the passive voice:

- After we receive the notices . . .
- You agree to pay the full purchase price . . .

These conversions to the active voice have a number of advantages. The sentences are shorter. The tone is direct and vigorous. The subject matter of the sentence is concrete and clear. And we have imposed a contractual obligation directly on an actor rather than left it floating—as if the obligated action would somehow simply happen.

Inappropriate passive-voice constructions abound in traditional legal drafting. Here are three real-world examples that struck me as particularly problematic because in each case, the passive voice construction fails to impose a contractual obligation on a party:

- All payments due before April 30, 2005, shall continue to **be sent** to the lender at the address set forth above. [Sent by whom?]
- Insurance coverage amounts or types must **be revised** to fully cover your property. [Who must revise them?].
- Permits **are to be secured** before construction of the residential pool can commence. [Who must secure the permits?]

Whenever it is possible to eliminate the passive voice and impose an obligation directly on one of the parties, you should do it.

Wordiness

When you can cut words and not lose meaning, do it. Shorter is better, as long as you don't lose content. Sometimes, a plain-English version of a text even ends up longer than the original, especially if you've inserted explanations of legal terms. Still, whenever you can, you should cut, cut, cut.

Things to look for:

nominalizations	using the verb form usually eliminates words
modifiers	*duly, applicable, expressly, further* (saying it directly is usually better)
general redundancies	*at this point in time* (now), *during such time as* (when)
legal redundancies	*cease and desist, above and foregoing, true and correct*
redundant lists	*sell, convey, and transfer* and *ordered, adjudged, and decreed*
legalisms	*pursuant to* (under), *subsequent to* (after), *in the event that* (if)

Here is an example of wordiness from some pattern jury instructions:

Original

Do not make personal inspections, observations, investigations, or experiments nor personally view premises, things, or articles not produced in court.

Some suggested revisions:

Original	**Suggestions**
Do not make personal inspections	Change the nominalization: *make personal inspections* becomes *inspect*
inspections, observations, investigations, or experiments	Consolidate the list by eliminating true redundancies or by using broader terms: Is *inspecting* truly different in this context from *observing*?

nor personally view premises	Cut unnecessary modifiers: Is there a difference between *personally viewing* and *viewing*?
things or articles not produced in court	Cut redundancies: Is there a difference between *things* and *articles*?

Revision

Do not view or inspect places or things from this case unless they are presented as evidence in court.

Punctuation

This isn't a comprehensive guide to punctuation, just a review of some important highlights for plain legal drafting.

Serial commas

Rather than discuss all the rules for commas, I would like to focus on one important comma in legal drafting: the serial comma.

For legal documents, always include a comma after the coordinating conjunction in a series of three or more items. Granted, this is a formal approach to writing; for informal writing, such as journalism and literature, the serial comma is often omitted. Still, even though you are writing legal documents for a nonlegal audience, you should adopt the more formal rule of always using the serial comma. The reason is simple, according to Bryan Garner: Omitting it can cause ambiguities, but including it never will.[4] In all the following examples, the serial comma is used correctly:

- Do not view premises, things, or articles not produced in court.
- The statement shall set forth the fees charged to the player for individual salary negotiations, management of players assets, and any other miscellaneous services.
- All claims, whether for money damages, penalties, or equitable relief shall be resolved by binding arbitration.

4. Bryan A. Garner, *A Dictionary of Modern Legal Usage* 714 (2d ed. Oxford Univ. Press 1995).

Many lawyers, particularly transactional drafters, resist using the serial comma. But because it eliminates confusion about whether the final two items in the series are one unit or two, its use is preferred. What's more, its absence has caused litigation. The following text was sent to me by a lawyer seeking to hire me as an expert witness. The text has other problems, but please notice that the last two items in this lengthy series are not separated by a comma (highlighted):

> "Cash" means cash, cash equivalents, other short term investments having a readily ascertainable market value, investments held in board designated funds, excluding, however, any such assets whose use is limited to payment of current liabilities, **all Trustee held funds and malpractice funds** . . .

The parties to this litigation were, in part, disputing whether "Trustee held funds" and "malpractice funds" were one thing or two things. I believe a transactional drafter, following a widespread but faulty convention, omitted the comma between the last two items. The revision would look like this:

> "Cash" means cash, cash equivalents, . . . all Trustee held funds, and malpractice funds . . .

If an appeal to authority will convince you, here it is:

- Put commas between all items in a series.[5]
- Always put a comma before the *and* or *or* in a series.[6]
- Use commas between items in a series.[7]
- Use commas to separate the items in a series.[8]
- Always use the serial comma.[9]

Semicolons

In legal drafting, the semicolon has primarily two uses:

5. Terri LeClercq, *Expert Legal Writing* 152 (U. Tex. Press 1995).

6. Robert J. Martineau & Michael B. Salerno, *Legal, Legislative, and Rule Drafting in Plain English* 68 (Thomson West 2005).

7. Anne Enquist & Laurel Currie Oates, *Just Writing: Grammar, Punctuation, and Style for the Legal Writer* 244 (2d ed., Aspen L. & Bus. 2005).

8. Richard C. Wydick, *Plain English for Lawyers* 88 (5th ed., Carolina Academic Press 2005).

9. Bryan A. Garner, *The Elements of Legal Style* 15 (2d ed., Oxford U. Press 2002).

1. it separates the items in a numbered list; and
2. it separates items in a series when one or more of the items has its own internal commas.

The two numbered items above show the first use. Even if the items in the series could be separated by commas, in legal drafting there is a convention to use the semicolon if you've numbered the items.

The second primary use of the semicolon prevents confusion about which are the main items in a series and which are subordinate or internal items embedded within the main items. Look at the following two examples; the original caused litigation that might have been avoided if it had been punctuated as in the revised example.

Original

"Cash" means cash, cash equivalents, other short term investments having a readily ascertainable market value, investments held in board designated funds, excluding, however, any such assets whose use is limited to payment of current liabilities, all Trustee held funds, and malpractice funds.

Revised

"Cash" means cash; cash equivalents; other short term investments having a readily ascertainable market value; investments held in board designated funds, excluding, however, any such assets whose use is limited to payment of current liabilities; all Trustee held funds; and malpractice funds.

I grant you that the text is now a little heavy on punctuation. But that is far better than the confusion and ambiguity that resulted from the use of commas alone.

Hyphens

When two words jointly modify a noun, the general rule is to connect the jointly modifying words with a hyphen. There are exceptions, of course, such as when the first word is an adverb or when the modifiers form a well-known stock phrase. Still, you'll enhance clarity and precision when you consistently hyphenate jointly modifying words. Here is our definition of "cash" again, with the needed hyphens supplied (highlighted):

> "Cash" means cash; cash equivalents; other **short-term** investments having a readily ascertainable market value; investments held in **board-designated** funds, excluding, however, any such assets whose use is limited to payment of current liabilities; all **Trustee-held** funds; and malpractice funds.

The use of the hyphen in this way is not as carefully practiced within the law as it should be. But well-written documents should use the hyphen this way. For example, all the following phrases were hyphenated in a single chapter of a law-related book:

law-school training
full-time teacher
second-class citizen
career-long pursuit
first-year course
law-review style
big-picture advice
law-firm library
professional-level text
in-house editor
large-scale weaknesses

Colons

In legal drafting, the colon primarily introduces lists. The standard and traditional convention is that the text before a colon should be an independent clause. That is, it should be a complete sentence, capable of standing on its own. But modern English and the conventions of legal drafting have changed this rule. Generally, it is acceptable to use a colon after almost anything, even a dependent clause or phrase.

As a practical matter, what this means is that more formal-sounding, lead-in sentences can be replaced with shorter phrases:

Correct but formal

"Cash" has the following meanings:

a. cash;
b. cash equivalents;
c. other short-term investments having a readily ascertainable market value; and

d. investments held in board-designated funds . . .

Also correct, but informal

"Cash" means:

a. cash; . . .

Dashes

The dash, or the "em-dash," as it is also known, is an entirely appropriate punctuation mark to use in legal drafting. It is particularly useful to emphasize parenthetical information when using parentheses would have a tendency to deemphasize the information. Please note that the dash—like those in this sentence—is the longest of the three horizontal punctuation marks, the others being the hyphen (-) and the en-dash (–).

You can also insert examples into a sentence with a pair of dashes, and the examples will then take on emphasis. This advice comes from Professor Paul Marx in his excellent book, *The Modern Rules of Style*,[10] and this example comes from a ticket I purchased:

Original

Holder consents to the search of all bags, packages, or any other container brought to the Museum or its premises.

Revision

You consent to the search of all personal items—bags, packages, or any other container—brought to the Museum or its premises.

Pay attention to your sentences, to their length and complexity. Pay attention to actors and use more of them. Pay attention to punctuation. These things matter, and your attention to them will pay off in clearer writing.

10. Paul Marx, *The Modern Rules of Style* 50 (ABA 2007).

CHAPTER 10

Using Readability Tests

Learn the appropriate uses for readability tests, then use them wisely.

Understanding readability scales

Readability scales are mechanical tests writers can use to get a sense of the readability of a piece of text. Probably the most well known of the readability scales is the Flesch Readability Scale, created by Rudolf Flesch. Flesch created his readability scale while doing graduate work at Columbia University. His first readability scale was based on several factors including "human" words (I, you, we) and vocabulary lists. He eventually simplified the test to measure average word length in syllables and average sentence length in words.[1]

There are other readability tests. The Dale–Chall formula was created in 1948 and updated in 1995. The Gunning Fog Index was

1. Rudolf Flesch, *How to Write Plain English: A Book for Lawyers and Consumers* (Harper & Row 1979).

created in 1952. The SMOG index was created in 1969.[2] But because Microsoft uses the Flesch Readability Scale in its Microsoft Word software, the Flesch Readability Scale is the most frequently used and well known.

Microsoft Word can calculate a Flesch readability score for any selected text. Go to Tools > Spelling and Grammar > Options and check the box that says "Show readability statistics." You may need to check the box that says "Check grammar with spelling" to get the readability-statistics function to work. This is too bad, because the grammar checker is not very good; I estimate that at least half of the things it tells me are just plain wrong. My solution is to click the button on the right that says "Settings" and then uncheck all the grammar boxes. The program is still "checking" your grammar, but it has been told not to check for anything.

When you assess the readability of your text in Microsoft Word, your computer compares your average sentence length and average word length to the Flesch scale. Because it relies on average sentence length and average word length, the Flesch scale punishes long sentences and long words. Of course, in legal drafting, sometimes long words are necessary. And of course, serious writers know that even long sentences can be quite easy to understand if they are well constructed. For these reasons, the Flesch scale is a limited tool.

That's why, on occasion, writing experts criticize the use of the Flesch scale, pointing out that it is a mindless word-and-syllable counter. It knows nothing about tone, style, or grammatical correctness. It cannot help you write correctly or in a way that makes sense if you don't already know how.

Of course, they're right. Take this sentence:

> Issued order the judge an.

It scores well on the Flesch scale even though it makes no sense. That's why readability scales are simply one tool to aid in plain legal drafting. They give you a sense of how understandable your text is, but they generally should not be an end unto themselves.[3]

For example, some states require that certain consumer documents score at certain levels on the Flesch scale. In Texas, at least

---

2. Mark Hochhauser, *What Readability Expert Witnesses Should Know*, 54 Clarity 38 (Nov. 2005).

3. William H. DuBay, *Smart Language: Readers, Readability, and the Grading of Text* 113 (2007).

three different kinds of consumer contracts will not be approved by regulating boards unless they score 40 or higher on the Flesch scale. Using a rigid numerical Flesch score may not be ideal, but it's better than letting lawyers prepare consumer documents without regard to readability.

Flesch readability scores range from 0 to 100, and Flesch himself said that a score of 60 constituted "plain English." For my money, any legal document that can score 50 or higher is pretty good.

Besides the Flesch scale, plain legal drafters can also use something called the Flesch–Kincaid formula, created in 1975. This formula, also available in Microsoft Word, applies a numerical grade level from 1 to about 20. The grade level corresponds to the number of years of post-kindergarten education a reader would need to comprehend the document. (By the way, versions of Microsoft Word before 2003 have a Flesch–Kincaid formula that is mistakenly capped at 12. So no matter how complex the writing is, it will not show anything beyond a 12th-grade reading level.) When you use the Flesch–Kincaid formula, you again get a general sense of the readability of the text.

Using readability scales

Rather than rely too heavily on any one readability assessment, I like to consider a number of factors when I seek to improve a piece of traditional legal writing.

First, I like to measure the before-and-after average sentence length. Long sentences are hard on readers, especially nonlawyers. We lawyers—having spent at least three years and often much longer reading statutes, judicial opinions, and briefs by opposing counsel—are used to long sentences. Nonlegal readers are not.

Second, I like to measure the before-and-after Flesch score. If I can move a document that originally scored in the 30s to a score above 50, I consider it a great improvement. I try not to get hung up on achieving a 60—Flesch's goal for plain English. Depending on the complexity of the subject matter, scoring 60 may be difficult or even impossible.

Third, I like to measure the before-and-after Flesch–Kincaid grade level. For complicated legal materials, I often aim for a grade level of about 10. My thinking is that if a 10th grader can understand what I'm writing, I'm doing a pretty good job. But I have taken complicated legal texts and converted them into simpler texts that have scored at a seventh- or eighth-grade level. (Note:

many of the readability scales use vocabulary lists that students of a certain grade level should know. Some of these lists haven't been updated since the 1940s.[4])

Here's a story that illustrates the appropriate use of readability scores and other factors in assessing the readability of a document.

I was once hired by a national bank to rewrite a series of consumer home-loan documents into plain English. At the same time, I provided training for lawyers at the bank, so they could begin redrafting the bank's basic deposit agreement into plain English. One of the senior attorneys at the bank, after completing my training, programmed her Microsoft Word to assess the average sentence length, Flesch score, and Flesch–Kincaid grade level. She then began to redraft a 14-page section of the deposit agreement into plain English.

The original text had the following traits:

Average sentence length:	42 words
Flesch score:	27 ("very difficult," according to Flesch)
Flesch–Kincaid grade level:	19

Pause for just a moment and calculate that grade level. That's right, it is a high school education—12 years—plus seven years of additional education. That's a college degree and a law degree. This assessment tells us this document was really aimed at lawyers.

But this lawyer assessed one other aspect of the document. She was able to program Microsoft Word to report on the percentage of sentences using the passive voice: the original had 50 percent passive-voice sentences. We've already seen that passive-voice constructions are a recurring problem in legal writing and can make legal writing dry, formal, and unnecessarily complex.

After she completed a rewrite of the 14 pages, applying the principles I suggested (which are the principles in this book), she reassessed those four aspects of the text. Here's what she found:

Average sentence length:	22 words
Flesch score:	57
Flesch–Kincaid grade level:	9

4. Mark Hochhauser, *What Readability Expert Witnesses Should Know*, 54 Clarity 38 (Nov. 2005).

Percentage of passive voice: 20 percent

Of course, the revised text could still have been nonsensical gibberish. But probably not. That's the job of a lawyer: Make the text understandable and grammatically correct. Assuming you have done that job, the numerical scores are a good indicator of how difficult a nonlegal reader would find the text (or how easy).

Thus, the readability scales are merely rough assessments that give you a numerical measure. They are tools. They help. But you should not let yourself become fixated on the Flesch score. (Believe me, I have become fixated on a few occasions. On one project I drove myself nuts trying to move the score from 59 to 60.)

Other cautions

Because word processors are not sophisticated human readers, their judgments about the readability of a piece of text are naturally limited. For example, if your document contains many legal citations, these will be construed as single or even multiple sentences, and they will inflate the Flesch score and push the sentence length down. Keep that in mind.

If your text contains topic headings, tabulated lists, and extensive numbering, you may again see your average sentence length drop artificially and your readability score rise. These are more good reasons to view the readability scales only as tools.

Some examples

Here are some before-and-after examples with their numerical assessments.

Original jury instructions

Do not conceal information or give answers which are not true. Listen to the questions and give full and complete answers.

Do not make personal inspections, observations, investigations, or experiments nor personally view premises, things or articles not produced in court.

If you do not obey the instructions I am about to give you, it may become necessary for another jury to re-try this case with all of the attendant waste of your time here and the expense to the litigants and the taxpayers of this county for another trial.

We shall try the case as fast as possible consistent with justice, which requires a careful and correct trial.

Average sentence length:	22 words
Flesch score:	50
Flesch–Kincaid grade level:	12

Revised jury instructions

Be honest when the lawyers ask you questions, and always give complete answers.

Do not view or inspect places or items from this case unless they are presented as evidence in court.

If you do not follow these instructions, I may have to order a new trial and start this process over again. That would be a waste of time and money, so please listen carefully to these instructions.

I assure you we will handle this case as fast as we can, but we cannot rush things. We have to do it fairly and we have to follow the law.

Average sentence length:	16 words
Flesch score:	77
Flesch–Kincaid grade level:	7

Original disclaimer

The holder is admitted on condition, and by use of this ticket agrees, that he will not transmit or aid in transmitting any description, account, picture or reproduction of the baseball game or exhibition to which this ticket admits him. Breach of the foregoing will automatically terminate this license.

The holder assumes all risk and dangers incidental to the game of baseball including specifically (but not exclusively) the danger of being injured by thrown or batted balls and agrees that the participating clubs, their agents and players are not liable for injuries resulting from such causes. The management reserves the right to revoke the license granted by this ticket.

Average sentence length:	27 words
Flesch score:	34 ("fairly difficult," according to Flesch)
Flesch–Kincaid grade level:	15

Revised disclaimer

This ticket admits you to the event listed on the front. By using it, you agree not to broadcast or help broadcast any descriptions or pictures of the event. If you do, you must leave the event.

By using this ticket, you accept the risks of attending a baseball game. For example, you could be hit by thrown or batted balls or injured in other ways. Stadium management, its representatives, the teams, and the players are not responsible for those injuries.

Management may revoke this ticket and remove you from the event.

Average sentence length:	13 words
Flesch score:	64
Flesch–Kincaid grade level:	7

If you have never used the Flesch Scale or the Flesch–Kincaid grade-level tool, you should try them. For all your legal writing, particularly writing aimed at nonlawyers, these numerical assessments can give you a sense of your effectiveness. Just remember that they are only tools.

For a thorough understanding of the Flesch readability scale, you should read Rudolf Flesch's book, *How to Write Plain English: A Book for Lawyers and Consumers.*[5]

5. Rudolf Flesch, *How to Write Plain English: A Book for Lawyers and Consumers* (Harper & Row 1979).

APPENDIX A

Before-and-After Texts

1. Before

Whereas, Attorney is about to undertake the performance of substantial legal services on behalf of the Personal Representative; and

Whereas, the State Bar's rules of professional conduct encourage attorneys and clients to enter into fee agreements; and

Whereas, the Probate Code requires that attorney fee agreements be signed by the personal representative;

Now therefore, in consideration of their mutual promises stated herein, the parties hereby agree that:

1. After

The Attorney is about to perform substantial legal services for the Personal Representative.

The State Bar's rules of professional conduct encourage attorneys and clients to have fee agreements.

The Probate Code requires that attorney fee agreements be signed by the Personal Representative.

Therefore, the parties agree as follows:

* * *

2. Before

This publishing contract is entered by Jackie Griffin (hereinafter "Griffin") and Evermore Computer Publishing House, Inc. (hereinafter "ECPHI").

2. After

This publishing contract is entered by Jackie Griffin and Evermore Computer Publishing House, Inc. Griffin and Evermore have agreed that Griffin will write and Evermore will publish a book aimed at the technology market. . . .

3. Before

THE HOLDER IS ADMITTED ON CONDITION, AND BY USE OF THIS TICKET AGREES, THAT HE WILL NOT TRANSMIT OR AID IN TRANSMITTING ANY DESCRIPTION, ACCOUNT, PICTURE OR REPRODUCTION OF THE BASEBALL GAME OR EXHIBITION TO WHICH THIS TICKET ADMITS HIM. BREACH OF THE FOREGOING WILL AUTOMATICALLY TERMINATE THIS LICENSE.

THE HOLDER ASSUMES ALL RISK AND DANGERS INCIDENTAL TO THE GAME OF BASEBALL INCLUDING SPECIFICALLY (BUT NOT EXCLUSIVELY) THE DANGER OF BEING INJURED BY THROWN OR BATTED BALLS AND AGREES THAT THE PARTICIPATING CLUBS, THEIR AGENTS AND PLAYERS ARE NOT LIABLE FOR INJURIES RESULTING FROM SUCH CAUSES. THE MANAGEMENT RESERVES THE RIGHT TO REVOKE THE LICENSE GRANTED BY THIS TICKET.

3. After

This ticket admits you to the event listed on the front. By using it, you agree not to broadcast or help broadcast any descriptions or pictures of the event. If you do, you must leave the event.

By using this ticket, you accept the risks of attending a baseball game. For example, you could be hit by thrown or batted balls or injured in other ways. Stadium management, its representatives, the teams, and the players are not responsible for those injuries.

Management can revoke this ticket and remove you from the event.

4. Before

TO: ALL RECORD AND BENEFICIAL HOLDERS OF THE COMMON STOCK OF ETRA, INC. (THE "COMPANY"), INCLUDING ALL OF ITS PREDECESSORS, DURING THE PERIOD BEGINNING ON AND INCLUDING JANUARY 1, 1995 THROUGH AND INCLUDING MARCH 22, 2007.

PLEASE READ THIS NOTICE CAREFULLY AND IN ITS ENTIRETY. YOUR RIGHTS MAY BE AFFECTED BY THE LEGAL PROCEEDINGS IN THIS LITIGATION. BROKERAGE FIRMS, BANKS, AND OTHER PERSONS OR ENTITIES WHO ARE MEMBERS OF THE CLASS IN THEIR CAPACITIES AS RECORD OWNERS, BUT NOT AS BENEFICIAL OWNERS, ARE DIRECTED TO SEND THIS NOTICE PROMPTLY TO BENEFICIAL OWNERS.

The purpose of the notice is to inform you of this lawsuit (the "Action"), a proposed settlement of the Action (the "Settlement"), and a hearing to be held by the Circuit Court (the "Court"), on October 5, 2007, at 1 p.m. (the "Settlement Hearing"), at which the Court shall consider for approval: (i) whether this Action will be certified as a class action, for settlement purposes only, pursuant to Rule of Civil Procedure 23; (ii) whether the terms and conditions of the Settlement are fair, reasonable, adequate, and in the best interests of the Class and the Company; (iii) whether the Final Order should be entered dismissing this Action with prejudice as against Plaintiffs and the Class, releasing the Settled Claims, and enjoining prosecution of any and all Settled Claims; (iv) the award of Plaintiffs' counsel's attorneys' fees and expenses as provided for herein, as to which award Company has agreed to pay $7.5 million; (v) any objections to the Settlement; and (vi) such other relief as the Court may deem necessary and appropriate. Any of the dates set forth herein may be modified by the Court without further notice. The Court reserves the right to approve the Settlement at or after the Settlement Hearing with such modifications as may be consented to by the parties to the Stipulation and without further notice to the Class.

THE DESCRIPTION OF THE ACTION AND THE SETTLEMENT WHICH FOLLOWS HAS BEEN PREPARED BY COUNSEL FOR THE PARTIES. THE COURT HAS MADE NO FINDING WITH RESPECT TO SUCH MATTERS, AND THIS NOTICE IS NOT AN EXPRESSION OR STATEMENT BY THE COURT OF FINDINGS OF FACT.

4. After

If you owned stock in Etra, Inc. between January 1, 1995, and March 22, 2007, you may have rights in a class-action lawsuit.

- **Read this notice carefully—it affects your rights.**
- **Brokers and agents: forward this notice to beneficial owners of Etra stock.**

This class-action lawsuit may be settled. This notice explains the details and how you can participate if you want to.

The judge will hold a hearing about the settlement on October 5, 2007. At the hearing, the judge will consider these things:

- whether to dismiss this lawsuit and prevent the plaintiffs from suing again;
- whether to approve this lawsuit as a class action;
- whether the settlement is fair, reasonable, adequate, and in the best interests of the class and Etra;
- whether there are any objections to the settlement;
- whether to give the plaintiffs' lawyers $7.5 million in fees and expenses—which Etra has agreed to pay;
- anything else the judge thinks is appropriate.

The judge can change the date without notice, and the judge can approve the settlement at the hearing or later. If the parties agree, the judge can change the details of the settlement without notice to the class.

The lawyers prepared this document, not the judge. **The judge has not made any decisions yet.**

5. Before

KNOW ALL MEN BY THESE PRESENTS, that I/we Linda Smith residing at 1000 Amber Lane, Emmett, ID, the undersigned, First Party, for and in consideration of the sum of FIVE THOUSAND AND NO/100 Dollars ($5,000.00) to me/us in hand paid by Real Insurance, Inc. and John James, Second Party, the receipt of which is hereby acknowledge, I/we being of lawful age, for myself/ourselves, my/our heirs, administrators, executors, successors and assigns hereby remise, release, acquit and forever discharge the said Second Party, his/her, their, and each of their heirs, executors, administrators, successors, and assigns and any and all other persons, partnerships, associations, and/or corporations, whether herein named or referred to or not, of and from any and every claim, demand, right, or cause of action of whatever kind and nature, either in law or equity, especially liability arising from an accident which occurred on or about 08/11/2005 at or near the following location INTERSTATE 100, DOWNTOWN, USA for which I/we have claimed the said Second Party to be legally liable, but this release shall not be construed as an admission of liability.

5. After

Form to release your claims.

Us:	Real Insurance, Inc. 250 Gray St. #500 Boise, ID	You:	Linda Smith 1000 Amber Lane Emmett, ID
Our insured:	John James		

By signing this release form, you give up all your claims against us and against our insured. In return, we will pay you $5000. The claims you are giving up are from an accident on August, 11, 2005 near Interstate 100, Caldwell, ID. We and our insured admit no liability.

You are giving up all your claims against us and any other person or company related to us. You are giving up all your claims for anyone else who might act for you or who might have rights through you.

6. Before

Player also shall reimburse Contract Advisor for all reasonable and necessary travel expenses actually incurred by Contract Advisor during the term hereof in the negotiation of Player's NFL contract, but only if such expenses and approximate amounts thereof shall be approved in advance by Player.

* * *

In performing these services, Contract Advisor acknowledges that he/she is acting in a fiduciary capacity on behalf of Player and agrees to act in such manner as to protect the best interests of Player and assure effective representation of Player in individual contract negotiations . . .

6. After

You agree to reimburse the Contract Advisor for all reasonable and necessary travel expenses the Contract Advisor incurs—related to negotiating your NFL contract—during the term of this agreement. The Contract Advisor must get your approval for the approximate amounts of those expenses in advance.

* * *

In performing these services, the Contract Advisor is acting in a fiduciary capacity—meaning with the utmost good faith—for you. The Contract Advisor agrees to protect your best interests and to represent you effectively in negotiating your NFL contract.

7. Before

Attorney is about to undertake the performance of substantial legal services on behalf of the Personal Representative, for which Attorney shall be paid fees and costs. The Personal Representative has retained Attorney to provide legal services to the Personal Representative for administration of the probate estate.

7. After

I am about to begin doing serious legal work for you. You have hired me to represent you in administering the probate estate. You will be paying my fees and costs.

8. Before

Therapeutic Recovery Care Hospital for Children ("TRCHC") has provided this web site for educational and informational purposes only. The material contained herein is believed to be complete and generally in accord with accepted standards at the time of publication. However, because of the possibility of human error and changes in medical science, TRCHC and its employees do not warrant that the information contained herein is in every respect accurate or complete, and thus, are not responsible for any errors or omissions or for the results obtained from the use of such information. TRCHC makes no representation or warranties, expressed or implied, and disclaims any liability for injury and any other damages which result from an individual using techniques discussed on this site.

8. After

We (the Therapeutic Recovery Care Hospital for Children and its employees) provide this website for education and information only. We believe the material here is complete and generally met accepted standards when we published it. But because people make mistakes and medical science changes, we don't warrant that the information is entirely accurate or complete. We aren't responsible for any errors or omissions or for the results if you use this information. We make no representations or warranties, expressed or implied, and we're not liable for injury and any other damages if you use techniques discussed on this site.

9. Before

Do not conceal information or give answers which are not true. Listen to the questions and give full and complete answers.

Do not make personal inspections, observations, investigations, or experiments nor personally view premises, things or articles not produced in court.

If you do not obey the instructions I am about to give you, it may become necessary for another jury to re-try this case with all of the attendant waste of your time here and the expense to the litigants and the taxpayers of this county for another trial.

We shall try the case as fast as possible consistent with justice, which requires a careful and correct trial.

* * *

You are instructed that you may not draw an adverse inference from the witness's claim of privilege.

9. After

Be honest when the lawyers ask you questions, and always give complete answers.

Do not view or inspect places or items from this case unless they are presented as evidence in court.

If you do not follow these instructions, I may have to order a new trial and start this process over again. That would be a waste of time and money, so please listen carefully to these instructions.

I assure you we will handle this case as fast as we can, but we cannot rush things. We have to do it fairly and we have to follow the law.

* * *

A privilege is the right not to testify. Do not assume anything when a witness uses a privilege.

10. Before

Reproduction of all or part of the contents of this page in any form is prohibited other than for individual use and it may not be recopied and shared with a third party. The permission to recopy by an individual does not allow for incorporation of this material or any part of it in any work or publication, whether in hard copy, electronic, or any other form.

10. After

You may not reproduce all or part of the contents of this page in any form—other than for individual use—and you may not recopy and share it with a third party. If we permit you to recopy, you may not put this material or any part of it into any work or publication, whether in hard copy, electronic, or any other form.

11. Before

"Cash" means cash, cash equivalents, other short term investments having a readily ascertainable market value, investments held in board designated funds, excluding, however, any such assets whose use is limited to payment of current liabilities, all Trustee held funds, and malpractice funds.

11. After

"Cash" means

(a) cash;
(b) cash equivalents;
(c) other short-term investments with a readily ascertainable market value;
(d) assets held in board-designated funds, but not any of those assets whose use is limited to paying current liabilities;
(e) all Trustee-held funds; and
(f) malpractice funds.

12. Before

On January 31, 2005, WyTech Sales, Inc. (the "Borrower") entered into an agreement with Nuttall Systems & Technology Transfer, Inc. ("NSTT") under which all of the Borrower's accounts receivable

("Receivables") of which you are the obligor have been pledged to NSTT. The Borrower has established a lockbox (the "Lockbox") for collection of Receivables. Accordingly, you are hereby instructed to remit all payments of Receivables of which you are, or have been, the obligor to . . .

12. After

This letter contains instructions for you to begin paying accounts you owe WyTech Sales, Inc. to Nuttall Systems & Technology Transfer, Inc.

Background

On January 31, 2005, WyTech Sales, Inc., the borrower gave Nuttall all its accounts receivable as collateral. You are the payer on some of these accounts. From now on, pay those accounts to a lockbox the borrower has established here: . . .

13. Before

IN THE UNITED STATES DISTRICT COURT
FOR THE EASTERN DISTRICT OF OKLAHOMA

JODY GRENDER,)
Plaintiff,)
)
v.) Civil Action No. CV-06-00985
)
CONSTANCE L. AMBLERTON,)
Commissioner,)
Social Security Administration,)
Defendant.)

DEFENDANT'S RESPONSE TO PLAINTIFF'S OBJECTIONS TO COMMISSIONER'S MOTION FOR ENTRY OF A JUDGMENT REVERSING AND REMANDING FOR FURTHER ADMINISTRATIVE PROCEEDINGS WITH BRIEF

13. After

United States District Court
Eastern District of Oklahoma

Jody Grender,	)	
Plaintiff,	)	
v.	)	Civil Action No. CV-06-00985
Constance L. Amblerton,	)	
Commissioner,	)	
Social Security Administration,	)	
Defendant.	)	

Defendant's Response to Plaintiff's Objections to Commissioner's Motion For Entry of a Judgment Reversing and Remanding for Further Administrative Proceedings

14. Before

NO. 07-28233-S

READY-FOODS INC.,	§	IN THE DISTRICT COURT OF
DRY-MADE, INC.	§	
Plaintiffs,	§	
	§	
v.	§	CHEROKEE COUNTY, TEXAS
	§	
SCHMIDT JONES L.L.P.,	§	
Defendant.	§	554th JUDICIAL DISTRICT

PLAINTIFFS' ORIGINAL PETITION

14. After

No. 07-28233-S

Ready-Foods Inc.,	§	554th Judicial District
Dry-Made, Inc.	§	
Plaintiffs,	§	
	§	
v.	§	Cherokee County, Texas
	§	
	§	
Schmidt Jones L.L.P.,	§	
Defendant.	§	

Plaintiffs' original petition

APPENDIX B

What Is Plain English?

Get informed and begin practicing the many principles of plain English.

I stated in the introduction that the goal of this book is to teach you how to write binding legal text so that nonlawyers can read and understand it. But what does it mean to write so that nonlawyers can understand? It means to write in plain English. So what is plain English? Defining plain English thoroughly would take this entire book. I take a stab at defining it briefly in this appendix, with nine plain-English principles. Then I recommend some excellent sources for further study. Finally, I debunk some common myths about plain English.

A caution about the word "plain": Do not let it lead you to believe that plain English is dull, drab, or boring. Rather, "plain English" simply means a form of English that is appropriate to its intended audience. It is a form of English that uses every tool at its disposal to make text clear, simple, and direct. But even though plain-English experts have been explaining that for many years, the concept of plain English is still sometimes criticized: "[Plain language] has a bad name among some lawyers. This is usually because they don't understand enough about it to judge it properly."[1]

Thus, the main criticisms of plain English come from the uninformed. You will not be one of them. Below are nine key principles for preparing legal documents in plain English in the order in which they appeared in this book.

The plain-English writing principles in this book

Know and write for the nonlegal audience (Introduction)

To communicate binding legal text effectively, you must be aware of the needs and limitations of the intended audience. To some extent you must forget you are a lawyer. Instead, you must think carefully about how to explain complex legal subjects in everyday language.

Master your forms—and question them (Chapter 1)

Much incomprehensible legal writing is handed down from previous documents, whether you prefer to call them forms, templates, guides, or precedents. Using forms is, of course, necessary for legal practice. Retaining the bad legal writing in the forms is not.

Design readable text: Manage type and lines; design accessible documents; use summaries, headings, and numbering (Chapter 2)

No one practicing law is using a typewriter, so everyone preparing documents for nonlawyers should take advantage of modern document-design principles. These enhance the accessibility and readability of legal documents.

Use consistent, modern writing and drafting conventions (Chapter 3)

Just because we are writing in plain English does not mean we can afford to be sloppy, inconsistent, and hasty. Learn and practice the modern rules of legal usage. These principles apply to traditional legal drafting as well as to plain-English legal drafting.

1. Michèle M. Asprey, *Plain Language for Lawyers* 11 (2d ed., Federation Press 1996).

Plan and execute a sensible organization with digestible, connected paragraphs (Chapter 4)

Think about what is important to the nonlegal reader and order your document accordingly. Think about the way typical readers use a document, then make it easy for them to skim your document, skip around in your document, and get key information quickly and easily.

Test documents on readers (Chapter 7)

You probably spent years in law school and law practice conditioning yourself to read and understand traditional legal writing. That's why no matter how hard you work, your first drafts will still probably not be ideal plain-English documents. You can improve them by seeking feedback from your readers.

Prefer concrete, direct, everyday words; abandon legalisms, archaisms, and Latinisms; speak to the reader (Chapter 8)

Pay attention to your words. Develop a sense of which words nonlawyers are familiar with, and use them. Likewise, develop a sense of which words are lawyer-speak, unnecessary terms of art, and unnecessarily formal. Avoid them.

Construct simple sentences with a 20-word average (Chapter 9)

Once you have sensitized yourself to vocabulary, take control of your sentences. Identify and avoid the traditional legal-writing habits that plague most legal sentences.

Learn to use readability scales wisely (Chapter 10)

Your word processor can become a tool to aid you in producing plain English. But you'll need to understand what readability scales do, how they do it, and what they cannot do. Once you know their strengths and limits, you can use them effectively.

The best sources on plain English

In writing this book, I have relied on the expertise of many lawyers and writing experts. Today you can find numerous excellent sources on plain-English writing in the law. Next, I offer my choices for the best books on plain English.

A Plain Language Handbook for Legal Writers by Christine Mowat

- This book takes a document-by-document approach to plain English and offers specific recommendations for each document. My favorite chapter is the one about wills, in which the author explains how she pushed her lawyer to prepare a plain-English will.

How to Write Plain English: A Book for Lawyers and Consumers by Rudolf Flesch

- After he worked as a consultant for the Federal Communications Commission, Rudolf Flesch, the creator of the Flesch Readability Scale, wrote this book about the work. His tone is enthusiastic and motivational, and his advice is practical.

Language on Trial: The Plain English Guide to Legal Writing by Plain English Campaign (Chrissie Maher)

- The author runs a nonprofit organization that pressures lawyers and legislators in England to use plain English. The book has lots of good advice and some excellent before-and-after examples.

Lifting the Fog of Legalese by Joseph Kimble

- Professor Kimble is the leading expert on plain-English legal writing in the United States today. This book collects his articles and columns on the subject. Kimble's tone is forceful and persuasive, and he backs up what he says with research.

Plain Language for Lawyers by Michèle M. Asprey

- Asprey works in Australia and is one of the leading plain-English proponents in that country. Her book has lots of examples of outrageously bad legal writing. She also has an excellent chapter on testing plain English.

Plain English for Lawyers by Richard C. Wydick

- This is one of the most successful legal-writing books of all time, widely used and recommended in American law schools. Its simple, straightforward approach makes it an excellent source for those who are interested in learning about plain English, and also for those who simply want to improve their own legal-writing style.

Plain and Accurate Style in Court Papers by Irwin Alterman

- Although this book is now more than 20 years old, it is in many ways still ahead of its time. Alterman tracked the Federal Rules of Civil Procedure and offered excellent recommendations for bringing plainness to court documents. The book's principles are still relevant today.

Securities Disclosure in Plain English by Bryan A. Garner

- Garner is the foremost expert on American legal usage. In this book he explains how to conform to the Securities and Exchange Commission's rules for plain English in prospectuses. The book is thorough and powerful. It also contains an example of a before-and-after prospectus as well as a copy of the SEC's own Plain English Handbook.

Writing Contracts in Plain English by Carl Felsenfeld and Alan Siegel

- This is one of the earliest books to focus on improving legal documents intended for nonlegal readers. The authors are a lawyer and a language expert. Much of the book focuses on three consumer documents: a consumer-loan note, an apartment-sale contract, and a personal-liability policy. This book encourages lawyers to write appropriately for the nonlegal audience. As the authors say: "The game of plain English is to make functional documents function."

Getting past the myths about plain legal language

Arm yourself. When someone tells you plain English won't work, rebut, respond, and press on.

By now you understand the basic principles of the plain-English movement: that legal writing intended for nonlawyers ought to be clear and readable to nonlawyers. But if you try to use it, you're bound to encounter resistance. Some resistance will come from others, but some of it will come from within you. You're a lawyer, after all, and you have subconsciously accepted some myths about "plain" legal writing. I aim to debunk them.

Some myths about plain English

1. Plain English requires brevity, which isn't possible in most legal documents.
2. Plain English requires a literary style that is not appropriate for legal writing.
3. Plain English lacks the precision of traditional legal language.
4. Plain English doesn't meet the expectations of clients.

Let's debunk these myths one at a time.

1. The truth: plain English doesn't require brevity, but it often produces it.

This image of plain English—that it is only about shorter words and shorter sentences—is the most common misunderstanding of plain English. In an article called *Against Plain English,* a law professor named David Crump captured the essence of this myth when he asserted that "there is the model in which plain English refers to the brevity of the expression."[2]

Not so. Brevity isn't really the goal; it's a benefit. Besides, plain English has many attributes besides brevity. Make no mistake: brevity is highly valuable, as David Lambuth said in *The Golden Book on Writing*: "The fewer the words that can be made to convey an idea, the clearer and the more forceful that idea."[3]

But we plain-English types don't say shorter is always better, and we never say you must achieve brevity at the expense of clarity or accuracy. In fact, we say the opposite. In her book *Plain Language for Lawyers,* the Australian plain-English expert Michèle Asprey says, "Brevity is one of the aims of plain language, but it is not the only one."[4]

2. David Crump, *Against Plain English: The Case for a Functional Approach to Legal Document Preparation,* 33 Rutgers L.J. 713, 728 (2002).

3. David Lambuth, *The Golden Book on Writing* 20 (Penguin Books, Ltd. 1983).

4. Michèle M. Asprey, *Plain Language for Lawyers* 306 (3rd ed., Federation Press 2003).

And Peter Butt and Richard Castle explain in *Modern Legal Drafting*, plain English accepts technical terms and "big" words if they are necessary: "While it shuns the antiquated and inflated word and phrase, which can readily be either omitted altogether or replaced with a more useful substitute, it does not seek to rid documents of terms which express important distinctions."[5]

Still, some lawyers believe this myth—that plain English requires shortening of all big words—and they offer these excuses:

Excuse: Many big words are necessary terms of art. True terms of art are only a tiny part of all legal writing, and the existence of a few terms of art is no justification for the vast majority of bad legal writing that requires no terms of art. Experts on legal writing and legal drafting have been saying this for years. In *Legal Drafting in a Nutshell*, Thomas Haggard says that "specific words or phrases that absolutely must be used to achieve a particular result are relatively rare."[6] And in *Legal Writing: Sense and Nonsense*, David Mellinkoff says that "[w]here lawyers mislead themselves, and everyone else, is in believing that most of the words they use are terms of art."[7]

Besides, plain English does not require us to drop all terms of art. It requires us instead to be sure that the word or phrase we are using actually is a term of art and that it is genuinely more precise than ordinary English.

Excuse: Explaining law in plain-English takes more words, not fewer. This is true, and far from being a criticism of plain English, it is one of its tenets. Plain-English advocates teach that unnecessary words ought to be cut and that a long word should be replaced when there is a shorter equivalent. But plain-English advocates reject pompous legalisms even if the everyday-English substitute is longer or requires more words.

Excuse: Legal language is specialized, so using ordinary words won't work. Professor James White raised this concern in his 1985 book, *Heracles' Bow*, when he said that the plain-English movement would never go far because when you replace a legal word with an

5. Peter Butt & Richard Castle, *Modern Legal Drafting: A Guide to Using Clearer Language* 85-86 (Cambridge U. Press 2001).

6. Thomas R. Haggard, *Legal Drafting in a Nutshell* 190 (West 1996).

7. David Mellinkoff, *Legal Writing: Sense and Nonsense* 7 (West 1982).

ordinary-English word, the law will eventually convert the ordinary word into a legal word.[8]

But the plain-English movement is about a lot more than words. In fact, plain-English advocates are so universally acquainted with this uninformed "simple words" criticism, that many try to preempt it by addressing it in their writing. Butt and Castle, for example, take plain English well beyond words: "[P]lain language is concerned with matters of sentence and paragraph structure, with organization and design, where so many of the hindrances to clear expression originate."[9]

Similarly, Kimble has offered this explanation in his article *Writing for Dollars, Writing to Please*: "[P]lain language is not just about vocabulary. It involves all the techniques for clear communication—planning the document, designing it, organizing it, writing clear sentences, using plain words, and testing the document whenever possible on typical readers."[10]

Thus, anyone who reads the literature on plain English learns that plain English is about more than simple words. Re-read the plain-English principles at the beginning of this Appendix. Notice that word length and sentence length are important but that they are not the only things mentioned.

This statement from Michèle Asprey ought to clear things up for good:

> Plain-language drafting is more than just a matter of using simple words. Less than half this book is devoted to words. The rest looks at writing for your audience, choosing the appropriate tone, planning, structure, design and layout, readability, devices to help your reader find things, testing, and some "philosophical" matters.[11]

2. The truth: plain English doesn't require literary style.

The myth holds that plain-English advocates want lawyers to write like Ernest Hemingway, or at least like a succinct novelist. Richard

---

8. James Boyd White, *Heracles' Bow: Essays on the Rhetoric and Poetics of the Law* 71-72 (Univ. Wisc. Press 1985).

9. Peter Butt & Richard Castle, *Modern Legal Drafting: A Guide to Using Clearer Language* 85-86 (Cambridge U. Press 2001).

10. Joseph Kimble, *Writing for Dollars, Writing to Please*, 6 Scribes J. of Legal Writing 1, 2 (1996–1997).

11. Michèle M. Asprey, *Plain Language for Lawyers* 197 (2nd ed., Federation Press 1996).

Hyland seems to be the one who set up this myth in his 1986 article *A Defense of Legal Writing*. He said that critics of traditional legal writing—the plain-English crowd—have "an idea implicit in their suggestions for improvement: namely that lawyers should write like novelists."[12] It's obvious why he had to say it was implicit. In reality, plain-English advocates don't say that at all.

In my experience, the only people who portray "literary style" as a goal of the plain-English movement are those who are criticizing plain English. That's what Professor Crump did in *Against Plain English*, in which he said that "rewriting a tested, proven formula into a more literary style, of one's own invention, is inadvisable."[13] But plain-English advocates do not suggest that lawyers rewrite their forms in a literary style. This argument is a straw figure that is too easy to knock down.

Granted, some experts say plain English can be enjoyable to read. But no legal-writing expert asserts that a loan agreement ought to be written like a Hemingway novel. Plain-English advocates temper the aspiration to write clearly and plainly with the realities of legal practice. For example, here is what Goldfarb and Raymond say in *Clear Understandings* about lawyers trying to write plainly:

> We are not so naïve as to suppose that lawyers should write like journalists or novelists, or that their prose should always be entertaining as well as instructive. On the other hand, we are persuaded that lawyers who have distinguished themselves as great writers have in common with other good writers certain techniques, certain resources, certain sensibilities to the nuances of language that enrich the law, not encumber it, making its expression both pleasurable and precise.[14]

As with the brevity myth, this misplaced criticism is common enough that experts have addressed it. In *Modern Legal Drafting*, Butt and Castle admit that "a legal document will never read like

---

12. Richard Hyland, *A Defense of Legal Writing*, 134 U. Pa. L. Rev. 599, 599 (1986).

13. David Crump, *Against Plain English: The Case for a Functional Approach to Legal Document Preparation*, 33 Rutgers L.J. 713, 725 (2002).

14. Ronald L. Goldfarb & James C. Raymond, *Clear Understandings: A Guide to Legal Writing* xv (West 1982).

a good novel, but it can be attractive and effective in a clean, clear, functional style."[15]

To say that plain-English advocates insist that legal writing be "literary" is to misunderstand the aims of the plain-English movement and to be ignorant of the literature on plain English. Legal-writing expert Mark Mathewson reiterates that point in a piece he wrote responding to Hyland. That piece is called *A Critic of Plain English Misses the Mark*, and in it Mathewson says this: "Lawyers should write like novelists? If that were truly what plain-language advocates thought, Hyland could rightly dismiss them, but that's not what they think, at least none that I've read."[16]

3. The truth: plain English doesn't lack precision.

This raises two related excuses for not writing in plain English: that traditional legal language is more precise than plain English and that traditional legal language is based on reliable precedent.

The precision excuse. This excuse is usually mentioned by lawyers and law professors as a stock response whenever someone calls for plain English. But it also shows up in print. Professor Crump perpetuated this excuse in *Against Plain English*. He asserted that traditional phrases are more precise than plain-English phrases.[17]

Anyone who challenges plain English on precision ought to carry out the following exercise. Pick a traditional legal word or phrase. Look it up in a legal-usage dictionary and in *Words and Phrases* (the West publication that collects judicially created definitions). Then figure out if the traditional legal word is really more precise than the ordinary word. Usually, it's not.

Those who challenge plain-English advocates on precision need to read Joseph Kimble's excellent article *The Great Myth that Plain Language Is Not Precise*. He says the choice is not between plain English and precision, because there cannot be perfect preci-

15. Peter Butt & Richard Castle, *Modern Legal Drafting: A Guide to Using Clearer Language* 95 (Cambridge U. Press 2001).

16. Mark Mathewson, *A Critic of Plain English Misses the Mark*, 8 Scribes J. of Legal Writing 147, 148 (2001–2002).

17. David Crump, *Against Plain English: The Case for a Functional Approach to Legal Document Preparation*, 33 Rutgers L.J. 713, 732 (2002).

sion in written English. So the choice is really between imprecise writing in plain English and imprecise writing in the dense fog of legalese.[18] Kimble prefers plain English, as do I.

More important, as Kimble asserts in *Writing for Dollars*, plain English and precision are complementary: "If anything, plain language is more precise than traditional legal writing because it uncovers the ambiguities and errors that traditional style, with all its excesses, tends to hide."[19] And Kimble presents, in both *The Great Myth* and *Writing for Dollars*, dozens of real-world examples of companies, government agencies, and individuals improving documents and saving money by using plain English.

Other experts agree. Butt and Castle say that

> [P]lain English is as capable of precision as traditional legal English. It can cope with all the concepts and complexities of the law and legal processes. The few technical terms that the lawyer might feel compelled to retain for convenience or necessity can be incorporated without destroying the document's integrity.[20]

The precedent excuse. The excuse of precision itself relies on another great excuse in legal writing. Those who say that traditional legal language is more precise than ordinary English rely on this venerated but questionable proposition: "Once legal language has been construed by a court, its meaning is clear; it ought to be set in stone."

Isn't it just as likely that the next judge, confronted with the same language in a different factual context, will say that it means something else? It's not too hard to figure out. Look through *Words and Phrases*. A few minutes in there ought to dispel the idea that judges are consistent in assigning meaning to legal language. Mellinkoff calls *Words and Phrases* "an impressive demonstration of lack of precision in the language of the law."[21]

18. Joseph Kimble, *The Great Myth that Plain Language is Not Precise*, 7 Scribes J. of Legal Writing 109, 116 (1998-2000).

19. Joseph Kimble, *Writing for Dollars, Writing to Please*, 6 Scribes J. of Legal Writing 1, 2 (1996–1997).

20. Peter Butt & Richard Castle, *Modern Legal Drafting: A Guide to Using Clearer Language* 95 (Cambridge U. Press 2001).

21. David Mellinkoff, *The Language of the Law* 375 (Little, Brown & Co. 1963).

Yet the precedent excuse—that courts construe legal words and give them reliable meanings—often goes unchallenged. Mellinkoff challenged the idea in *The Language of the Law* in 1963. And he convincingly debunked the idea that litigation-tested language makes good form book material.[22]

In my view, Michèle Asprey got it right: "So how comfortable should we feel when we say that a word has years of case law behind it which tells us what it meant? Surely what we are actually saying is that people have been arguing over its meaning in various contexts for years."[23]

4. The truth: clients don't prefer legalese.

Writing in a traditional, dense, and archaic legal style is sometimes treated as a full-employment plan for lawyers. If clients could understand what we write, some say, they wouldn't need the lawyers. This thinking relies on some questionable premises.

Excuse: Clients take legalese seriously because it's impressive. Clients do take some legalese seriously. The legal linguist Peter Tiersma suggests in his book *Legal Language* that "in the courtroom, verbal formulas and ritualistic words put the audience on notice that this is a proceeding with important consequences." But he goes on to question the value of this formal language more generally: "Even though formal legal language may serve some purpose, we should ponder whether that goal might not be carried out just as well by some other means, one that does less injury to the goal of clear communication."[24]

After all, it is the legal effect of words, not their emotional impact, that is important in most legal writing. Of course, jury arguments and persuasive briefs are a different matter. But if a drafted document says what it legally needs to say, even in simple terms, a court should enforce it.

Besides, are clients really impressed with traditional legal language? Generally, no. Here's what two nonlawyer writing experts

---

22. David Mellinkoff, *The Language of the Law* 278-82 (Little, Brown & Co. 1963).

23. Michèle M. Asprey, *Plain Language for Lawyers* 24 (3rd ed., Federation Press 2003).

24. Peter M. Tiersma, *Legal Language* 102-03 (Univ. Chicago Press 1999).

have to say about lawyers' justifications for traditional legal writing:

> [W]e outsiders are not persuaded. We suspect that lawyers use the old language at times because it is conveniently available in form books, or because it makes them sound like lawyers, or because they are blissfully unaware of how odd it really is, or because they think it will fill us outsiders with awe and a willingness to pay handsomely for documents beyond our ken. We even suspect that on occasion lawyers themselves do not understand the language of the law.[25]

Excuse: Clients expect and prefer traditional legal language. I haven't met a client who has said this. Only lawyers say this, on behalf of clients. Is it true? I doubt it.

In one study conducted in Australia, nonlawyer clients reported that understanding what a lawyer had written for them was important: "These people said they wanted their lawyers to give them practical, commercial advice which they could actually use to solve their problems—and they wanted it in plain language."[26] These clients, at least, seemed to prefer plain English to traditional legal language.

Plain-English advocates and drafting experts today remind lawyers again and again that we must try to draft documents—as much as possible—so that nonlawyer clients can understand them. Michèle Asprey writes that "We cannot continue to pretend that legal writing is meant to be read and used only by lawyers."[27] And Howard Darmstadter suggests a new model for preparing legal documents: "A legal document should teach a reader how a transaction works."[28]

---

25. Louise Mailhot & James D. Carnwath, *Decisions, Decisions . . . A Handbook for Judicial Writing XIV* (Les Éditions Yvon Blais 1998).

26. Michèle M. Asprey, *Plain Language for Lawyers* 68–69 (2d ed., Federation Press 1996).

27. Michèle M. Asprey, *Plain Language for Lawyers* 8 (3rd ed., Federation Press 2003).

28. Howard Darmstadter, *Hereof, Thereof, and Everywhereof: A Contrarian Guide to Legal Drafting* 25 (ABA 2002).

Today, more and more clients want to know what their lawyers are doing for them, and they are willing to find a new lawyer who can explain things clearly. More and more clients have gotten the notion that if you're a professional, you should be able to explain complex matters in plain terms.

Still, some lawyers believe that they will put themselves out of business if they do not write complicated documents; they believe, according to Robert Dick, that a "client comes to the office to receive a lengthy, magic document of the deepest obscurity."[29] But Dick, in his book *Legal Drafting*, questioned this theory: "Why obscurity should promote a lawyer's practice is difficult to understand. . . . Modern clients reject this approach and are no longer impressed with the hocus-pocus."[30]

In fact, many clients deride the traditional approach. Carl Felsenfeld and Alan Siegel, in *Writing Contracts in Plain English*, recognized that "ponderous language may create an illusion of precision. Among lay readers, it invites ridicule."[31]

And finally, more and more lawyers are realizing that traditional, convoluted legal drafting does not retain clients—it pushes them away. According to Peter Butt and Richard Castle: "Few things have done more to drive people from our doors than our inability both in documents and in letters and speech to express ourselves in clear simple English."[32]

Plain-English advocates aren't blind zealots. We acknowledge the value of terms of art, of form books, and of certain solemn legal language. We understand that all of those things have their places, but we insist that those places are small. Those limited uses should not be allowed to override the need to change legal writing in almost every other area.

Plain-English advocates also believe that clear and plain legal writing brings respect, appreciation, and clients.

---

29. Robert C. Dick, *Legal Drafting in Plain Language* 6 (3d ed., Carswell Co. 1995).

30. Robert C. Dick, *Legal Drafting in Plain Language* 6 (3d ed., Carswell Co. 1995).

31. Carl Felsenfeld & Alan Siegel, *Writing Contracts in Plain English* 144 (West 1981).

32. Peter Butt & Richard Castle, *Modern Legal Drafting: A Guide to Using Clearer Language* 91 (Cambridge U. Press 2001).

INDEX

ABOUT THE AUTHOR

Wayne Schiess is the director of legal writing at the University of Texas School of Law in Austin. He teaches legal writing, legal drafting, and plain English and is a frequent seminar speaker on those subjects. He has published more than a dozen articles on practical legal-writing skills, and three other books: *Writing for the Legal Audience, Better Legal Writing,* and *The Legal Memo: A Basic Guide*. In 2007, his blog, *Legalwriting.net,* was named one of the *ABA Journal*'s top 100 law-related blogs.

He also works as a consultant for those trying to simplify their legal documents. He has been a member of the Texas Pattern Jury Charges Plain-Language Task Force and has worked as a plain-English expert for a national bank, a home-construction company, and a community-access television provider.

He graduated from Cornell Law School, practiced law for three years at the Texas law firm of Baker Botts, and in 1992 joined the faculty at the University of Texas.